Swipe, Click, Love

The New Art of Dating

By
Reese D. Gallagher

Swipe, Click, Love

The New Art of Dating

Table of Contents

Introduction

In the digital age, the pursuit of love has transformed into an adventure unlike any our ancestors could have imagined. Once upon a time, finding romance was about chance meetings in a crowded café or through mutual friends. Today, it's an intricate blend of technology, psychology, and a touch of serendipity. The modern dating landscape is a vibrant tapestry of opportunities and challenges, shaped and reshaped by the devices in our hands.

Technology has carved a new narrative in the story of love, one where dating apps serve as gateways to an array of possibilities just a swipe away. Yet, this accessibility comes with its own set of complexities. We now navigate a world where messages replace murmured words, and emojis attempt to capture our nuanced emotions. How do we adapt to this whirlwind of communication, ensuring genuine connections and authentic experiences in an often dissonant digital world?

Within this book, we embark on a journey to untangle the web of modern dating. We aim to understand not only how technology has altered our romantic endeavors but also how we can wield it as a tool for fostering meaningful relationships. Despite the dizzying pace of technological advancements, the essence of love—connection, understanding, and intimacy—remains a timeless pillar.

The allure of digital dating lies in its promise of endless potential. We've become explorers in a vast landscape of profiles and personalities, each one a universe of its own. Yet, with this expansion comes a paradox of choice. The abundance of options can lead to overwhelming decision fatigue, leaving many of us wondering if the next swipe might reveal a better match or if we're missing out by staying put.

In navigating this terrain, the art of crafting an effective personal narrative becomes paramount. Our profiles act as digital storefronts, offering glimpses into our worlds. Crafting them with care and authenticity can mean the difference between superficial scrolling and sparking genuine interest. But how do we ensure our virtual selves align with our true identities without getting lost in the whirlwind of online personas?

As we delve deeper, we'll explore the psychological underpinnings of swiping, the chemistry that can transcend screens, and the nuances of virtual attraction. This book will guide you through the labyrinth of messaging, highlighting how to turn a simple "hi" into deeper, more engaging exchanges. Moreover, we'll touch upon the etiquette of online interactions—those unspoken rules that govern the success or failure of our digital pursuits.

Beyond the mechanics of online interactions, we'll address the emotional landscape of digital dating. Anxiety, pervasive and often unacknowledged, can hinder our interactions and hold us back from potential connections. Understanding this anxiety and learning strategies to overcome it will be a crucial focus, empowering you to approach dating with confidence and courage.

The pivotal transition from online to offline can often be the most daunting step. We'll offer insights on how to navigate this shift smoothly, ensuring that the connection that promises so much online blossoms into something meaningful in the real world. From planning that crucial first date to ensuring a lasting first impression, we aim to equip you with the tools to seamless transitions.

In an increasingly connected world, long-distance relationships are more common than ever. Yet maintaining the spark across miles can be challenging. This book will explore how technology can help bridge these distances, offering innovative ways to nurture and support love that wants to flourish despite the miles.

At the intersection of romance and technology lies a deeper query into the authenticity of our connections. We must ask ourselves: Are we connecting on a superficial level, or do our interactions hold genuine substance? This book encourages you to strike a balance, embracing technology without allowing it to overshadow the authenticity that forms the bedrock of true intimacy.

For those disenchanted by digital dating, we'll revisit traditional methods of meeting people, often overlooked but still valuable in their simplicity and potential for genuine connection. Bringing forth these timeless techniques can offer a refreshing break from the screen and open doors to unexpected possibilities.

The modern dating narrative isn't without its challenges, from the pressure of choice to the often ambiguous signals sent through our digital devices. Navigating these complexities requires patience and a keen sense of discernment. We'll explore how to read between the lines and understand the messages conveyed through words unsaid.

The digital world also presents unique challenges regarding diversity and inclusion. Celebrating different perspectives and addressing discrimination will be themes woven throughout this book, ensuring that every reader feels valued and empowered to seek love in an open, accepting environment.

Mindful dating practices will ground our discussions, reminding us of the importance of being present in this fast-paced world. Emotional intelligence, once a soft skill, becomes an essential part of modern dating, influencing our interactions and relationships profoundly.

In recognizing red flags and learning to listen to our instincts, we tap into a vital component of safe and successful dating. This book seeks to enhance your intuition and build your trust in your judgment, ensuring that your path in the digital dating world is both fulfilling and secure.

Finally, amidst cultural shifts and evolving norms, the support of therapy and self-reflection finds its place in the narrative of modern relationships. Recognizing when to seek guidance can be the key to unlocking personal and relational growth, offering new perspectives and paths forward.

As we thread through the complexities and beauty of modern dating, "Introduction" serves as the gateway to all that lies ahead in this book. It lays the foundation for a detailed exploration of how technology and romance intertwine, offering insights, strategies, and inspiration for anyone navigating the intricate pathways of love in the digital age.

Chapter 1:
The Evolution of Romance

In the dance of hearts through history, romance has always found ways to adapt to the changing landscape of human connection. From the sweet anticipation of hand-written love letters, cherished for their tangibility, to the immediate thrill of today's digital messages, technology has continuously reshaped the way we meet, fall in love, and maintain relationships. The essence of love, once captured in the aroma of a sealed envelope, now flows through the silent signals of swipes and texts. Yet, at its core, romance remains an unchanging quest for meaningful connection, negotiating the space between timeless emotion and digital innovation. As we journey through this first chapter, we explore how these shifts reflect not just the evolution of our interactions but also the profound adaptability of the human heart in its pursuit of love.

The Impact of Technology on Love

In today's rapidly evolving landscape, technology has fundamentally transformed the way we perceive and experience love. Once rooted primarily in face-to-face interactions and chance meetings, romance now thrives in a digital realm where boundaries of time and space blur effortlessly. Our smartphones, tablets, and computers have become the new confessional booths, secret gardens, and dance floors of courtship. The pervasive influence of technology challenges us to reimagine love, urging us to find genuine connections amidst screens and algorithms.

Technology enables love to blossom in spaces that were once merely fantasies. Video calls bridge oceans, allowing partners to maintain a semblance of intimacy with just a click. It's the era of love letters on steroids—text messages sent across time zones with ease. This digital communication not only sustains relationships separated by distance but also enriches them by encouraging continuous dialogue. By transforming separation into a quality time spent conversing and sharing, technology adds layers to the modern experience of romance.

Yet, this digital romance comes with its own set of challenges. One notable aspect is the paradox of choice. Dating apps present a seemingly infinite array of potential partners, each swipe offering a new opportunity. But with this abundance can come indecision and a fear of missing out. The array of choices can lead to a kind of analysis paralysis, where the search for 'the one' becomes endlessly self-defeating. Despite these challenges, technology inspires a compelling shift in mindset, one that encourages us to focus on personal growth and the quality of our connections rather than sheer quantity.

Technology also serves as a unique bridge across cultures and communities, broadening the horizons of whom we can love and how. It's a channel through which different worlds can collide and coexist. This democratization of romance means that we are freer than ever to pursue relationships that defy traditional boundaries. While obstacles still exist, especially for certain communities, digital spaces provide a platform for voices and narratives that might have been marginalized in more conventional arenas.

What's particularly transformative is the role technology plays in enhancing our emotional vocabularies. Emojis, GIFs, and voice memos become nuanced expressions of emotion, allowing us to convey more than words might. These tools help us articulate feelings that are sometimes difficult to express in person, fostering deeper connections and understanding. However, they also demand a new kind of literacy—one that involves reading between the lines and understanding the unspoken cues embedded within streams of digital communication.

In the quest for meaningful connections, we often find that authenticity becomes the ultimate goal. With the veil of anonymity that the digital world can offer, authenticity can be both elusive and powerful. Successful modern romances lean heavily on being genuine, a truth that technology both complicates and simplifies. On the one hand, screens can create distance, making it easier to hide or embellish reality. On the other, the anonymity can encourage openness, allowing individuals to reveal parts of their personality that they may be too shy or hesitant to expose in person.

Then there's the phenomenon of social media, shifting the public and private spheres of love. It allows us to share, celebrate, and sometimes scrutinize our relationships in a public forum. The act of posting parts of our love lives demands a careful navigation of boundaries and intentionality about which parts to share and which to keep sacred. This level of visibility can enhance a relationship by offering a community of support, but it can also introduce stress and pressure to maintain appearances.

With the wonderful tapestry that technology creates, there's the undeniable need for mindfulness—an awareness of how we integrate digital tools into our romantic experiences. It's about recognizing their influence, setting boundaries, and making conscious choices to foster genuine connections. At the heart of the digital romance is the age-old narrative of love itself, timeless and evolving, just as humans have always been. Remember, technology is a means, not an end, and it's the choices we make with it that define our experiences and connections.

In this new age of romance, technology offers both the canvas and the brush. It's not just about making love convenient; it's about making it deeper, enriching the tapestry of human connection with vibrant threads of communication and shared experience. By embracing these changes and adjusting our expectations, we can craft a digital dating life that's both fulfilling and authentic. Just as centuries ago, when people adapted to the advent of letters instead of verbal courtship, today we find ourselves adapting again, navigating a landscape that's at once unfamiliar and thrillingly full of potential.

From Letters to Texts: A Historical Perspective

As we journey through the ever-changing landscape of romance, it's essential to understand how communication has evolved over time. From love letters sealed with wax to text messages punctuated by emojis, each era has crafted its unique language of love. It's a story of innovation, adaptation, and sometimes nostalgia. Over centuries, the way we express affection and desire has transformed, reflecting both societal changes and technological advancements.

In ancient times, lovers relied on messengers carrying handwritten letters. These letters weren't just a means of communication; they were embodiments of thought and emotion, crafted over days, sometimes weeks. Every stroke of the quill spoke volumes, and the moment a lover's received the letter was filled with anticipation and heartfelt suspense. There was something undeniably romantic about this form of communication — a tangible connection through ink and parchment.

Fast-forward to the 19th century, and the love letter still held its ground, but it became more accessible to broader society. The invention of the affordable postal system contributed significantly to the popularization of letter writing among the middle classes. This era saw the birth of intimate correspondences like the famed exchanges between Elizabeth Barrett and Robert Browning, whose passion unfolded across pages. These relationships blossomed with every carefully selected word, reflecting a dance of intellect and longing.

With the advent of the telephone in the late 19th and early 20th centuries, love and courtship took another turn. No longer bound by geographical distances, people's voices could reach their beloved's ears instantly. The emotional cadence of one's spoken words could now carry the weight of love beyond the limitations of text. Phone calls allowed suitors to express themselves with immediacy and spontaneity, strengthening connections in a way letters could not.

The telephone brought with it new romantic conventions. Lovers no longer had to wait days for a response; they could engage in back-and-forth exchanges in real-time. Yet, this instant communication also demanded a new etiquette. The world was adjusting to the pros and cons of such immediacy, learning the art of crafting words without the safety of revision. Every call held the potential for both delight and disaster, depending on how adept one was at improvisation.

Then came the era of the Internet, which revolutionized how we find partners and express our feelings. In the late 20th century, the surge of emails introduced another shift. Email added efficiency while still retaining the written word's intimation. People could now send virtual letters with a click, complete with the nuances of love and desire but without the sentimentality of a tangible letter.

Email kicked open the doors to online dating platforms, initially hesitated upon but quickly embraced. Conversations moved to chatrooms and instant messaging. Love letters became digital snippets exchanged over Yahoo Messenger or AOL Instant Messenger, leading us to yet another reinvention of courtship. Texts emerged as the dominant medium in the early 21st century — now the default form of communication between potential and existing partners.

Text messages encapsulate what lovers of previous ages could only dream of: immediacy, spontaneity, and the ability to converse on-the-go. The brevity of text messaging encouraged a certain playfulness; emojis rose to prominence, serving as a succinct way to convey complicated feelings. An emoji can be worth a thousand words, and emoticons became vital in expressing irony, humor, or admiration quickly and effectively.

There are, of course, challenges. The lack of tone in texts can lead to misunderstanding, especially where romance is involved. A simple "Okay" can be read in myriad ways, prompting uncertainty and second-guessing. The power of an ellipsis or the absence of punctuation can lead to protracted internal dialogues about intent. We have adapted, incorporating learned nuances, and continue to develop strategies to convey emotion as efficiently as possible.

It's also worth noting the role of social media platforms and dating apps in further evolving digital courtship. Platforms like Instagram, Facebook, and Twitter began allowing individuals to share everyday moments, thus integrating them into their partner's lives in a more comprehensive manner. Here, love once again took center stage, providing a new setting where people curated and expressed their affections in more varied forms, blurring lines between private and public intimacy.

Understanding this historical evolution offers insights into the complexities of modern romance. It's not just about finding new ways to communicate love but also navigating the subtle intricacies that come with each technological advancement. It's about balancing traditional expressions of affection with the immediate demands of the digital age, and recognizing the value of both deep, reflective exchanges and spontaneous, fleeting conversations.

As we move forward, the challenge remains: How do we honor the depth of our feelings in an era that demands speed and efficiency? By examining the past, we can better appreciate the profound impact of how we communicate, and strive for connections that are not only instant and convenient but also deeply genuine.

Chapter 2:
Navigating the World of Dating Apps

In today's fast-paced world, dating apps have transformed the way people seek love and connection, introducing a new era of romantic exploration. These digital platforms offer a dynamic landscape where swipes, matches, and chats weave a tapestry of possibilities, blending serendipity with algorithmic precision. Navigating this realm requires both an open heart and a strategic approach, transforming profiles into compelling narratives that resonate authentically. Each platform boasts unique features, encouraging users to dive into a melting pot of personalities and preferences. But beyond the screen, it's the essence of real human connection that remains the ultimate prize. Here lies the challenge and the magic—balancing the allure of virtual flirtation with the pursuit of genuine intimacy, crafting a journey where romance can blossom in the most unexpected ways. Embracing this tech-enabled adventure requires courage and curiosity, as daters learn to dance with both innovation and intuition, exploring digital avenues in the quest for something truly meaningful.

Popular Platforms and Their Unique Features

As we delve into the intricate world of dating apps, it's clear that not all platforms are created equal. Each offers unique features tailored to different dating needs and preferences. These distinguishing characteristics can greatly influence the user experience, catering to a diverse array of romantic pursuits. Whether you're seeking a serious relationship or just looking to have some fun, there's an app that fits those desires.

Let's begin with **Tinder**, arguably the most iconic dating platform today. Known for its swipe-right-to-like interface, Tinder revolutionized how we approach dating. With ease of use and an enormous user base, it possesses a 'quick match' ethos that may appeal to those who enjoy spontaneity. The app's straightforward mechanism is based primarily on geolocation, providing users with potential matches nearby. However, beneath its seemingly casual surface, Tinder has also been successful in helping users find long-term partners.

In contrast, **Bumble** offers a unique twist by allowing only women to initiate contact after a match. This feature is designed to empower women in the dating realm, shifting typical dating dynamics and encouraging respectful interactions. Bumble's emphasis on female-first communication resonates with those who value safety and control in their online interactions. Furthermore, the app has expanded its purposes to include Bumble BFF for friend-making and Bumble Bizz for professional networking, showing versatility beyond romantic pursuits.

For those seeking something more profound, **eHarmony** stands out with its comprehensive approach to matchmaking. Unlike other platforms, eHarmony requires users to complete a detailed compatibility quiz. This thoroughness isn't for everyone, especially those who are more inclined towards fast-paced dating. However, it caters well to individuals earnest about finding a compatible partner for a serious relationship. The algorithm-driven matches focus on deep connections, significantly different from the quick swipe left or right methodology.

Additionally, **OkCupid** offers a blend of the traditional and contemporary by focusing on both personal depth and usability. Known for its extensive questionnaires, OkCupid uses a matching algorithm that considers users' likes, dislikes, and values. This data-driven approach positions it as a platform for those who appreciate a mix of science and serendipity in dating. With its strong emphasis on inclusivity, OkCupid provides numerous gender and orientation options, making it an appealing choice for people across the spectrums of identity.

Then there's **Hinge**, which markets itself on the promise of connecting people who are "meant to be deleted" — suggesting real, meaningful connections that might move users off the app. Hinge encourages users to interact based on engaging prompts rather than aimless swipes, adding a conversational depth to initial interactions. It integrates personality and wit right from the start, emphasizing a more interactive and thoughtful first impression.

Moving into the realm of niche dating platforms, **Raya** has gained attention as the app for elite and creatives. Its exclusivity stems from its invite-only status and a vetting process. This makes Raya appealing to individuals seeking privacy and an escape from the chaotic, open-access nature of traditional apps. For those intrigued by the idea of meeting people within specific professional fields or interests, Raya's allure is significant.

Grindr plays a pivotal role as the leading app for gay, bi, trans, and queer people. It's known for providing a sense of community and connection beyond just dating. Emphasizing chat capabilities that allow users to interact instantly, Grindr has created a space where physical proximity often translates into swift meet-ups, catering specifically to its audience's preferences and lifestyles.

Similarly, **HER** emerged as a dedicated space for queer women, emphasizing community over styled fast connections. HER champions inclusivity and engagement, hosting vibrant online and offline events. This platform extends beyond dating, functioning as a social network dedicated to queer women and non-binary individuals, encouraging users to connect over shared experiences and interests.

Understanding these platforms requires looking not just at the demographics they cater to, but the specific features they offer. From match algorithms and connection styles to safety measures and user interactions, these elements shape how we navigate digital love landscapes. By considering our preferences and intentions, we can choose a platform that aligns closely with our romantic aspirations, thus maximizing our chances of finding fulfilling connections.

What becomes apparent when exploring the multitude of options is how technology adapts to our ever-evolving understanding of relationships. Each app could be seen as a microcosm of society's diverse expectations, desires, and negotiations. By selecting the right platform and using its features effectively, individuals open up new avenues for potential love and companionship, navigating the digital world armed with both optimism and strategy.

Creating an Effective Profile

In the vast expanse of the digital dating landscape, your profile is your first impression. It's your chance to shine, to stand out, and most importantly, to be truly yourself. Crafting an effective profile goes beyond just a few flattering photos and generic descriptions. It's about authentic portrayal and strategic communication.

Your profile should be a reflection of who you are, capturing your essence in a way that's both genuine and attractive. It's not just about showcasing your best self, but also about being open about what you're genuinely looking for. While it might be tempting to embellish or tweak details for a glossier portrayal, authenticity builds the foundation for lasting connections.

First things first: your photos. They serve as the window into your world. While selecting the perfect pictures, think about showcasing a variety that reflects different facets of your life. A balance of a warm, inviting headshot, an action shot showing a hobby or passion, and maybe a candid moment with friends can tell a compelling story. Remember, a picture speaks a thousand words, so choose ones that open doors to a conversation. Avoid over-filtering or using old photos; truthfulness here sets realistic expectations and fosters trust.

Once you've curated your visuals, it's time to dive into the narrative: your bio. The goal here is to create a portrait of yourself that piques interest. Tell stories rather than listing facts. Instead of "I love hiking," maybe say, "There's nothing like reaching the peak of a sunrise mountain trail." Be concise but evocative. Let your words illustrate who you are, convey your interests, and hint at the subtleties that make you uniquely you.

Humor can be your secret weapon. A touch of well-placed wit invites engagement and showcases personality. A self-deprecating joke can signal confidence and approachability. But it's also important to gauge the humor in a way that feels natural to you. Forced jokes or canned humor can come across as disingenuous.

Beyond the basics, answering profile prompts when available can be your opportunity to let your quirks and individualities shine. Be real about what you're seeking, whether it's adventure, companionship, or a deep, romantic connection. It's these details that help others to envision what being with you might be like. Don't shy away from specifics; they weed out those not aligned with your path.

As you fine-tune your profile, consider the tone. Think of it as a personal conversation, inviting and open rather than formal or distant. Write as if you're speaking directly to the person you're hoping to meet. Authenticity is magnetic; it tends to attract those on the same wavelength.

A crucial yet often overlooked aspect is the quality of language. Clear, well-punctuated sentences signal that you care about how you present yourself. Proper grammar isn't about being snobbish; it's about ensuring clarity. Typos or slang that feels forced can detract from the professionalism and earnestness of your profile.

When detailing what you enjoy or the type of person you're seeking, try to strike a balance between specificity and openness. While you want to attract those who align with your interests, focusing excessively on rigid criteria may narrow your chances of unusual, enriching connections. Allow space for surprise and serendipity.

Your checklist should also include checking your profile from other devices. Sometimes, things may look different on an app versus a computer screen. Ensure that no photo is cropped awkwardly and that your text remains inviting everywhere it might be read.

Once your profile is active, periodic reviews and updates can keep it fresh and relevant. As you grow and your experiences evolve, so too should the narrative you share with potential matches. Updating your profile with new pictures from recent adventures or revisiting your bio to include recent achievements can keep you in the present and open to new possibilities.

Remember, in a world where first impressions are often filtered through a digital lens, your profile is your story, your painted canvas. Allow it to speak truths only you can tell, and in doing so, extend an invitation for genuine connection. It's about initiating relationships that are built on the likeliness of real-world encounter hardwired with digital potentials.

The beauty of creating an effective profile lies not merely in attracting the right swipes but in laying a foundation for meaningful connection. So, craft it with care, clarity, and character. The digital world is vast, but the path it offers can lead to relationships as real and rewarding as those formed across any café table or shared sunset.

Chapter 3:
The Psychology of Swiping

In the intricate world of dating apps, the simple act of swiping has unlocked a fascinating psychological dance, where each left or right motion plays a symphony of neurotransmitters in the brain. This instant gratification from potential matches often stimulates a burst of dopamine, creating addictive patterns similar to those seen in slot machines. Yet, with every high comes the risk of swift fatigue, as users grapple with the paradox of choice and the mental strain that comes with it. In navigating swipes—each one symbolizing both possibility and rejection—daters learn to balance desire with discernment. Here, understanding the psychological wiring can empower individuals to make mindful decisions, transforming aimless swiping into a purposeful path toward genuine connections.

The Dopamine Effect

Imagine this: you're cozied up on the couch, phone in hand, and your thumb is moving expertly across the screen. Each swipe left or right delivers a faint buzz, a simple cue for your brain that something engaging is happening. This motion, facilitating a world of possible connections, isn't just a mechanical one; it taps into something deeper—our brain's pleasure center. Welcome to the dance of dopamine, an inherent part of our modern dating ritual.

At its core, dopamine is a neurotransmitter, a chemical messenger crucial for transmitting signals in the brain, playing roles in how we feel pleasure and reward. It's the fuel for our drive and motivation. And when it comes to dating apps, dopamine is a big player. It's what keeps you coming back for more swipes, more matches, and more messages. The sleek design of the dating interface isn't by chance; it's meticulously crafted to engage your senses and, quite literally, your brain's reward pathways.

This might sound like science fiction, but it's a reality grounded in behavioral psychology. When you receive a match or even anticipate that possibility, dopamine is released. It's much like the feeling you get when finding the last cookie in the jar—unexpected and delightful. That little jolt of happiness? It's dopamine saying, "Here, have a little reward for your effort." And so, the cycle continues.

One might wonder how this cycle might influence our behavior. With each swipe, the anticipation grows—a simple movement holding the promise of endless possibilities. The power of choice is exhilarating, yet it can also be overwhelming. Each new face holds a story untold, a potential connection waiting to be unraveled. In this seemingly infinite sea of profiles, dopamine subtly convinces us that the next swipe could lead to "the one," keeping us hovering at the edge of discovery. It whispers that the next profile might be more interesting, more engaging, or more compatible.

The influence of dopamine isn't just limited to the swipe itself. It extends to the conversations that follow a match. The thrill of a notification, announcing a new message, stirs curiosity and encourages engagement. This cycle of reward and anticipation isn't unique to dating apps; it's seen in various facets of life, from scrolling through social media to checking emails. Yet, in the realm of dating, where personal connection and validation intertwine, its impact feels particularly potent.

While dopamine can indeed lead to engaging interactions and even fun, it also comes with its set of challenges. With so many potential matches available, the paradox of choice rears its head. You're faced with the possibility of choice overload, where too many options might make it harder to commit to one person. Here, dopamine can be a double-edged sword—both rewarding and relentless. The little dopamine hit you get might tempt you to keep looking, pushing for a better match or a more engaging conversation.

In fact, the very features that engage us most might sometimes drive us into a loop of dissatisfaction. It's a delicate balance between leveraging dopamine's potential to enhance our digital dating experience and recognizing when it becomes overwhelming. The art lies in understanding our brain's responses and navigating them with a sense of self-control and insight.

The good news? By becoming aware of this dopamine-fueled dynamic, we can take steps to cultivate healthier digital habits. Setting boundaries, like time limits on app usage or intentional swiping sessions, can help keep our interactions meaningful. It's about harnessing dopamine's positive effects without letting it dictate our every move in the digital dating landscape.

We might resist the pull of a new match or message for a moment by pausing, checking in with ourselves, and remembering our ultimate goals in seeking connection. Is it about the thrill of a match, or are we genuinely looking for someone to share our lives with? This self-awareness can empower us to turn dopamine's delightful dance into a journey towards truly fulfilling connections.

Ultimately, the trick is to enjoy the enchanting energy dopamine brings to digital dating, while also steering our inner compass towards authentic connections. It's balancing the exhilarating with the earnest—the dance of dopamine with the sincere search for love. As we navigate this journey, we find that the real magic isn't just in the brain chemical itself, but in how we choose to respond to it, converting fleeting digital interactions into meaningful connections.

Decision Fatigue in Dating

The dawn of the smartphone era has introduced us to a world that never quite powers down. Nowhere is this more evident than in the realm of modern dating, where single souls, swayed by the promise of love and connection, find themselves awash in a sea of potential partners. The swiping, tapping, and scrolling are incessant—an activity almost as mindless as brushing one's teeth in the morning. Yet, behind these swift technological gestures lurks a phenomenon that can profoundly influence our abilities to choose: decision fatigue.

Imagine browsing through a menu where every item looks delectable, but each bears a striking resemblance to the next. Which do you choose? In a similar vein, dating apps splay an array of profiles, each user vying for attention with a carefully crafted image and witty bio. At first, the options seem thrilling, a veritable buffet for the heart. However, after a stretch of engaging with countless profiles, the brain starts to tire, much like deciding on the hundredth dish in an endless feast.

Decision fatigue emerges when the act of making choices begins to wear down our mental and emotional faculties. As users wade deeper into dating apps, the abundance of options can paradoxically become overwhelming, making it harder to differentiate between contenders who genuinely pique interest and those who are mere distractions. This relentless cycle can lead to a corrosive sense of indecisiveness, or worse, the avoidance of making a choice altogether.

Consider a point in the dating app experience when swiping becomes mechanical, induced by the sheer volume of profiles. It's not merely a taps-and-texts issue. When the brain is overwhelmed by constant decision-making, it defaults to the easiest possible judgments, sometimes at the expense of more reasoned, deliberate choices. The appeal fades, and what once appeared empowering now feels like a burden. It's akin to standing at a busy crossroads, unsure of which direction to turn, and opting to stand still instead.

Drained by decision fatigue, it's easy to swipe right less selectively. Matches become more a function of chance than desire, connections forged on the whims of compromised judgment rather than genuine chemistry. The repercussions could be subtle, as simple as an overlooked potential match, or more pronounced, like a string of unfulfilling encounters that erode one's enthusiasm for dating altogether. This emotional toll can be significant, leading to frustration and questioning one's compatibility in the digital dating landscape.

To combat decision fatigue, it's essential to reintroduce mindfulness into the madness. One effective strategy is setting specific intentions before diving into the app—a form of mental preparation that clarifies what you're truly seeking. This mindset guides your digital journey, helping filter through the noise and focus on profiles that align with your authentic desires. It raises the importance of valuing quality over quantity, reminding the earnest seeker that fewer matches, carefully chosen, can lead to more meaningful interactions.

Limiting the window of time spent on the app can also make a difference, turning what can be a guilty pleasure into a purposeful pursuit. Allocating designated time slots for swiping—like a meeting with oneself—instills a sense of discipline, freeing one from the tyranny of infinite scrolling. It transforms a marathon of browsing into refreshing sprints, an approach that helps preserve the joy and anticipation of discovering new connections.

Moreover, incorporating breaks in the app-usage routine is vital. These pauses offer a chance to reflect on and evaluate the interactions thus far. Ask yourself: Are candid conversations developing organically? Is there excitement building around any particular connection? Reflection not only curtails the numbing effect of back-to-back swipes but also fosters intuitive awareness about who feels right for you.

Learning to listen to intuitive cues or gut feelings without dismissing them becomes another ally in decision-making. Often these instincts can cut through the noise of myriad choices. They are the intuitive whispers that prompt you to swipe left on a picture-perfect profile or encourage revisiting one you've previously skipped. Trusting oneself—especially in the face of bombardment by countless options—aligns selections with authentic preferences and helps mitigate fatigue.

It's also essential to engage in self-care practices outside the realm of digital interactions. Engaging hobbies, exercise, or time with friends can replenish the emotional reserves depleted by the taxing process of decision-making on apps. Grounding oneself in real-world connections and experiences enriches one's ability to connect virtually without the process becoming exhaustive.

The path through the digital dating landscape is illuminated not just by the glow of the screen, but by the realization that the heart and mind work best when liberated from undue stress. Decision fatigue underscores the challenge of choice, yet offers an opportunity for self-discovery and methodical engagement that aligns with individual values and desires.

By recognizing the presence of decision fatigue and consciously adapting strategies to manage it, individuals can navigate the dating world with renewed clarity. It's about reclaiming the art of connection, one thoughtful choice at a time, steering away from the clamor of endless possibilities towards the serenity of sincere human bonds.

Chapter 4:
Virtual Connections and Chemistry

The digital landscape offers new pathways for connection, where chemistry isn't just reserved for face-to-face encounters. In the virtual world, it's about establishing an emotional resonance that can transcend screens and bandwidth. You might wonder if two people can truly connect online, and the answer lies in the essence of interaction, not the medium. Through thoughtful messages and shared experiences, individuals can cultivate an authentic connection that feels as palpable as an in-person meeting. Building virtual attraction involves more than just swiping right; it requires curiosity, empathy, and vulnerability. In this ever-evolving domain, the chemistry sparked by words and digital exchanges has redefined the way we perceive romantic potential, encouraging us to embrace these virtual bonds with an open heart and a curious mind.

Can You Really Connect Online?

In the sprawling universe of online dating, a question persists: Can genuine connections spark from pixels and digital interactions? This query delves deep into the fabric of modern love. As mobile screens and keyboard strokes become our matchmakers, the traditional notion of chemistry faces a new challenge. But the mystery and allure of connection remains unchanged. Virtual or otherwise, it beckons us with its promises and perils.

Human connection thrives on the unspoken—a glance, a touch, shared laughter echoing across a room. In the digital realm, most of these cues vanish, leaving behind only words, emojis, and video calls. Yet, millions around the globe are forging relationships that are as steadfast and vibrant as those birthed in the physical world. There's something magical about words on a screen translating into heartbeats that sync.

Why, then, do online connections sometimes feel lacking? The answer isn't straightforward. In some cases, it's the absence of physical intimacy. In others, it's the overwhelming sea of options, which can make commitment seem daunting. Yet, perhaps the most significant factor lies in our expectations. We crave the instant spark, the fairy tale perception of love, which can sometimes overshadow the slow-building warmth of true affection.

And yet, magic happens online. Relationships that start with a simple "hello" have blossomed into lifelong commitments. How? It begins with authenticity. When you're building an online relationship, it's essential to transcend beyond the facade. No filters, just you. Engage genuinely, share your quirks, and let your personality illuminate the conversation. This realness fosters deeper connections that can withstand the transition from online to offline worlds.

Consider the power of storytelling. Sharing stories bridges gaps and builds empathy, allowing individuals to step into each other's lives, if only for a moment. In the digital dating realm, storytelling elevates mere conversations to deeper dialogues, fostering a virtual connection that mimics the intimacy of in-person exchanges.

Moreover, the written word offers a unique advantage. It allows us to craft our thoughts, deliberately engage, and even reflect before responding. This deliberation can nurture intimacy in ways spontaneous conversations sometimes fail to do. For those who find face-to-face interactions intimidating, the digital pause provides space to express thoughts more thoughtfully.

Online platforms today are designed to enhance virtual bonds. Features like video chats and interactive games deepen engagement, making digital experiences richer and more personal. These tools, when used mindfully, can serve as bridges to genuine bonding. When both parties are committed to understanding each other, even a thousand-mile separation can feel like a mere footstep.

Yet, beneath the warmth of connections, challenges loom. Misunderstandings can arise from tone misinterpretation, messages can be left on "read," and the occasional ghosting can cast a shadow over one's confidence. To truly connect, one must approach these challenges with resilience and open communication.

Also crucial is the understanding that online chemistry doesn't guarantee real-world compatibility. It's a starting point, but the journey requires courage. Bridging the gap from online to offline involves vulnerabilities—voice calls, video chats, and, eventually, face-to-face meetings. Encountering someone in the flesh means adapting to unfamiliar dynamics, body languages, and energies.

Trust also plays a vital role. The anonymity of the web can mask intentions. So, fostering trust over time is essential. Communicate openly about comfort levels, future prospects, and meet-up plans. Sharing these discussions builds a foundation that supports a healthy transition to offline encounters.

Finally, allow room for serendipity. While algorithms make predictions about compatibility, the unpredictable spark often defies logic. Enjoy the journey, embrace the digital landscape's spontaneity, and remember that a genuine connection often blossoms unexpectedly.

Can you really connect online? The answer is complex yet hopeful. Virtual connections demand the same ingredients as physical ones—honesty, empathy, and effort. While technology serves as a conduit, the true magic lies in the human spirit's unyielding ability to relate and love, even across screens. So, dive into the digital tide, seek those connections, and know that the possibility for warmth, understanding, and love is always a heartbeat away.

Building Virtual Attraction

In a digital landscape where swipes and clicks determine potential love, building virtual attraction has become an art form that combines both instinct and strategy. Unlike the physical world where a glance or a touch can spark interest, online attraction requires a different set of cues and interactions. Let's delve into how to ignite that initial spark and nurture it into a meaningful connection.

At its core, virtual attraction starts with the presentation of a digital self. Crafting a genuine and appealing presence involves more than just selecting flattering photos or writing a witty bio. It's about curating an authentic image that resonates with who you truly are. The challenge is to convey depth and personality in a space limited to text and images. An engaging profile captures attention and encourages potential partners to want to know more.

Just as in face-to-face interactions, first impressions online are crucial. The key is to express authenticity without overwhelming a prospective connection with excessive or irrelevant detail. A well-thought-out profile acts as both a filter and a magnet, attracting those who share your interests and values while repelling those with different priorities. This requires a combination of honesty, creativity, and sometimes a bit of humor to keep things interesting.

The subtleties of communication play a pivotal role in building attraction online. Words become powerful tools, carrying vibrations that can either intrigue or deflate. Messaging offers a unique venue to connect; it gives you the opportunity to consider your words carefully and deliver them with intent. Starting with delightful banter and gradually shifting into deeper conversations can bridge the gap between digital and emotional connection.

Active listening, although different in an online context, is just as important as when you're in someone's physical presence. Paying attention to what's shared, asking insightful questions, and responding thoughtfully enriches digital dialogues. This creates a narrative continuity that steadily builds rapport. In a space where distractions are frequent, maintaining focus on one conversation at a time can make all the difference.

The nuances of humor should not be underestimated when forging virtual attraction. A well-timed joke or a shared laugh can create an immediate bond. However, humor can be subjective and vary widely between individuals. Testing the waters gently with light humor can pave the way for discovering shared comedic sensibilities, which often enhances the connection.

Images, too, hold tremendous power in the realm of virtual attraction. While they can't replace the magnetism of physical presence, images can offer glimpses into lifestyles, hobbies, and personalities. Pictures should tell stories or evoke emotions, serving as conversation starters. Each image is a window into your world, so choose those that authentically represent you and complement your narrative.

Yet, building attraction isn't solely about presentation. Emotional intelligence subtly threads through the foundations of digital chemistry. Tuning into your emotions and those of others can guide interactions. Understanding how online behaviors influence feelings allows for more meaningful engagements and decreases misunderstandings.

Patience is a virtue, especially when building attraction online. Just as depths of connection deepen over time in the physical world, virtual chemistry also requires a gradual unfolding. Instant gratification can be tantalizing but fostering a connection that matures with patience often leads to more stable and rewarding bonds. It involves a cycle of nurturing interest, sharing intimacy, and growing together emotionally even across screens.

Barriers of distance and time zones vanish in the virtual space, providing endless opportunities to connect with individuals from diverse backgrounds. This diversity introduces richness and complexity but also demands adaptation and openness. Embracing differences and learning from each other ensures a vibrant interpersonal tapestry, filled with exploration and shared growth.

The courage to be vulnerable, even from behind a screen, can also strengthen virtual attraction. Sharing fears, dreams, and aspirations creates intimacy and trust, two elements crucial in transitioning from attraction to deep connection. The art lies in maintaining enough mystery to keep engagement while being open enough to invite genuine bond formation.

Virtual attraction, in all its nuances, transforms the way we perceive and engage in modern relationships. It offers the exciting possibility to connect across boundaries and shape relationships that thrive on emotional resilience and mutual understanding. As we continue to navigate this digital era, the challenge and opportunity lie in evolving how we build, define, and nurture those sparks into enduring human connections.

Chapter 5:
The Art of Messaging

In the swirling dance of digital connection, mastering the art of messaging is where the melody often starts to crescendo. It's here, in the space between crafted words and spontaneous bursts, that potential relationships first unfurl. Crafting messages thoughtfully can transform simple exchanges into powerful conduits of genuine emotion and intrigue. Every message sent holds the promise of new discovery, a delicate balance between revealing just enough and leaving room for wonder. The secret lies in understanding that while the medium is modern, the essence of connecting remains timeless— attentiveness, sincerity, and curiosity never go out of style. It's not just about saying the right thing; it's about saying it in a way that resonates deeply, inviting the recipient into a dance of minds and hearts poised with anticipation in this modern romantic arena.

Crafting the Perfect First Message

So you've swiped right and matched with someone who seems intriguing. That initial rush of excitement can quickly turn into a daunting question: What do you say first? Crafting the perfect first message isn't just a science; it's an art grounded in authenticity, intuition, and a sprinkle of charm. Your opening words essentially serve as the first impression, and as the old adage goes, you never get a second chance to make a first impression. This opening message sets the tone for future interaction and lays the groundwork for a potential connection.

It's tempting to fall back on clichés or resort to messages that are safe and unoriginal like a simple "Hey" or "What's up?". While these might feel like baseline conversation starters, they often lead down an unimaginative path. In a world saturated with superficial conversations, standing out requires something extra. It's about sparking curiosity, prompting intrigue, and evoking a genuine smile on the other side of the screen.

Personalization is the secret ingredient to crafting a memorable first message. Think of it like a bespoke gift tailored to that person's interests or something fascinating about them. Why mention the universe when their profile mentions they're a star-gazer? A personalized message not only shows you've paid attention but also fosters an immediate sense of connection. It portrays that you're genuinely interested and that the match wasn't just an accidental slip of the thumb.

Humor can be a fantastic ally if wielded correctly. A witty comment might break the ice, but be cautious—humor is subjective, and a misfired joke could hinder progress rather than help it. Finding a light-hearted reference to something they've mentioned on their profile is often a safe yet playful approach. The key is to strike a balance between being amusing and being respectful.

Authenticity is vital too. In an era where everything can feel filtered and ultra-curated, sincerity is refreshing. An authentic touch adds warmth to your message and makes it resonate on a deeper level. Confidently sharing a bit about yourself in the first message also opens the door for two-way communication. Instead of focusing entirely on the other person, integrate aspects of your identity—whether it's a shared love for hiking or excitement for an upcoming art exhibit.

Another essential aspect of a great first message is asking questions. Questions indicate a willingness to engage, showing that you're ready to listen and learn more about the other person. Open-ended questions work wonders as they require more than just a yes or no response, facilitating an engaging and lively conversation. This is your chance to transform the message from a monologue into a dialogue.

At times, start your message with a shared connection if possible. Maybe you both love the same book or band or have lived in the same city. This common ground can weave a sense of familiarity and comfort into your conversation, even when you're still digital strangers. It creates an invisible thread of shared experience that can frame early interactions.

Timing and tone also play crucial roles. Match the tone of your message to the tone you perceive in their profile. If they appear light-hearted and humorous, mirror that vibe. If they seem more serious or intellectual, offer a thoughtful or insightful first message. In terms of timing, sending a message promptly after matching can demonstrate enthusiasm, but don't rush it if you're struggling for the right words. Reflection can often lead to crafting a more impactful message.

Don't overlook the power of a compliment, but ensure it's genuine and specific. Compliments that go beyond the surface show depth of thought and can create a supportive, positive atmosphere from the get-go. Instead of stating the obvious about appearance, comment on something unique about them—perhaps their adventurous spirit as evidenced by their travel photos, or their engaging write-up in the bio section.

Lastly, remember that there are no foolproof formulas, given the unique dynamics of human interactions. It's about playing with words, crafting moments of connection, and sometimes, embracing the imperfections that come with trying to know a stranger. Each first message should be viewed as a canvass where you can leave an imprint that's personalized, approachable, and memorable.

In the end, the perfect first message boils down to being genuine, observant, and creative. While there might be bumps along the journey, focusing on authenticity and being attentive can help you craft a message that not only sparks a conversation but also lays the groundwork for a potential genuine connection. So go ahead, break the ice with confidence and a touch of flair, opening the door to new possibilities and companionships waiting on the horizon.

Maintaining Engaging Conversations

In the vibrant world of digital dating, conversation is the lifeline of any budding relationship. It holds the power to kindle deeper connections or extinguish potential joy before it even begins. Just as a craftsman hones his skills to create something beautiful, mastering the art of maintaining engaging conversations can transform a series of digital exchanges into a genuine relationship that feels invigorating and profound.

So, what makes a conversation truly engaging? At the heart of every engaging conversation is the principle of reciprocity—a balanced give and take, where neither party dominates nor retreats excessively. When one person listens as much as they speak, it becomes an exchange, a dance of words and ideas where both partners feel heard and valued. Sounds simple enough, but achieving this balance in the quick space of digital messages often requires both subtlety and skill.

The cornerstone of maintaining a lively conversation often lies in asking open-ended questions. Instead of settling on queries that can be met with a simple "yes" or "no," delve deeper. Consider asking questions that evoke stories or invite opinion, like "What's been the highlight of your year so far?" or "How do you find joy in the everyday?" These inquiries open doors to learn about your partner's experiences, values, and aspirations without assuming or expecting a particular answer.

However, questions alone can't sustain a conversation. Injecting your own stories and thoughts turns the dialogue into a shared experience rather than an interview. Sharing relatable stories and insightful personal anecdotes provides pathways for connection and adds texture to the digital text. It's in these stories that your personality truly shines, transforming a static line of text into a vivid image of who you are and what you believe in.

In the same way that conversations weave through our lives, emotional intelligence weaves through a successful digital exchange. Recognizing emotional cues and responding with empathy can elevate a mere conversation to a meaningful interaction. Acknowledging their emotions, using phrases like "It sounds like that meant a lot to you" or "I appreciate your honesty," can create threads of emotional resonance that intertwine, building a tapestry of trust and understanding.

The tempo of conversation is equally crucial. Messages that flow too quickly might overwhelm and those too slowly could render the exchange stagnant. Finding a comfortable rhythm that respects both your partner's availability and your own is key. Humor and light-hearted banter often play critical roles too. A well-timed joke or a playful tease can lift spirits and convey warmth, yet it's important to gauge your partner's receptivity and avoid comments that could be misinterpreted.

Moreover, embracing vulnerability can sometimes be the magic ingredient. Saying what's genuinely on your mind, even if it feels a little risky, can break down barriers and foster a deeper connection. It might be as simple as admitting that you're excited about meeting someone new or confessing your nerves about the first date.

Authenticity can strip away unnecessary complexity, laying the foundation for a relationship grounded in honesty.

It's not just about the content of your conversations, but also about continuity. Following up on previous topics, like asking how a friend's job interview went or if they enjoyed the event they were excited about, signals care and investment in their life. It shows that you listen and remember, which in turn builds goodwill and rapport.

This blend of storytelling, empathy, humor, and vulnerability requires practice and attentiveness. Some people may possess a natural flair for it, while others develop it over time. However, what goes unspoken can be as powerful as what is talked about. Silence and pauses, when used thoughtfully, can emphasize points or offer space for contemplative responses, deepening the flow and texture of the conversation.

Despite all the deliberate efforts, there's an aspect of spontaneity and unpredictability that keeps conversations fresh and engaging. Having the conviction to let the conversation sometimes meander without a fixed agenda can lead to surprising discoveries about each other—a mutual exploration that might uncover peculiar likes, shared dreams, or even unresolved past mischiefs.

Finally, it helps to remember that while you might aim for depth and thoughtfulness in your digital exchanges, perfection shouldn't be the goal. Successful conversations aren't about curating perfect content or crafting impeccable responses. They're about creating a space where both individuals feel comfortable to explore, express, and ultimately, connect.

Maintaining engaging conversations in the digital dating cosmos is a skill that effectively blends art and heart. With thought and patience, these conversations have the potential to nurture connections that extend beyond screens and lead to equally enriching encounters offline. As you explore these connections in your journey of love and companionship, let the art of conversation be your guide, helping to weave your individual stories into a joint narrative filled with meaning and possibility.

Chapter 6:
Online Flirting and Etiquette

In the world of digital romance, online flirting acts as both an art and a science, blending charm with technology. As our screens become portals to potential, understanding digital etiquette becomes crucial. The key to successful online interactions lies in balancing playfulness and respect; emojis can add a touch of fun, while carefully chosen words convey sincerity. It's all about reading between the lines—deciphering a witty quip or the subtle pause in a conversation. The dos and don'ts of digital communication aren't just about following rules but about creating a connection that feels both genuine and refreshing. By practicing empathy and patience, and indulging in curiosity rather than judgment, one can navigate this virtual dance, laying the groundwork for deeper connections that move gracefully from the screen to the heart.

Reading Between the Lines

In the dance of digital romance, much of what's communicated is found not just in words themselves but in the silences between them. Online flirting is an unspoken language, as much about what isn't said as what is. Being able to read between the lines is a skill that can reveal subtleties and complexities in digital interactions. It's the art of understanding intentions, desires, and emotions woven through the digital tapestry, often beyond the explicit text displayed on the screen.

The lack of vocal tone, facial expressions, and physical gestures in online interactions creates a unique challenge: interpretation. This is where reading between the lines becomes crucial. The tone of a message is derived not from sound but from word choice, punctuation, and timing. A simple "hey" could range from enthusiastic to indifferent, depending on whether it arrives peppered with exclamation marks, ellipses, or tempered by a delayed response. Here, emojis and GIFs play their roles, acting as the digital substitutes for gestures and expressions, adding layers of meaning that words alone might fail to convey.

Yet, even with these additions, digital flirtations demand a heightened sense of intuition. Someone's propensity to respond in emojis might express playfulness or mask uncertainty. A message sent at 2 AM versus one sent during a lunch break can reflect different levels of spontaneity or intent. These cues are vital for understanding the dynamics at play and deciphering underlying messages. Often, hesitation can be read in delayed responses, just as eagerness might be perceived in rapid replies.

Dating in the digital age requires paying attention to the flow of conversation and recognizing variations that might suggest deeper meanings. An abrupt end to a lively banter or subtly altered phrasing can hint at a change in mood or interests. It's where familiarity with one's correspondent becomes a guiding light. When you're comfortable with someone, you start picking up on these subtleties instinctively, translating and responding to them almost unconsciously.

An essential part of reading between the lines is the understanding of boundaries and respect for digital etiquette. It's recognizing when a playful nudge might be crossing into uncomfortable territory for the other person. What might seem like a flirtatious overture to one could be an imposition for another, highlighting the need for empathy and considerate communication. Acknowledging context is critical; the environment and prior conversations precede the nuances embedded in current exchanges.

This delicate dance also involves recognizing when someone might be holding back. The reluctance to dive deep into personal topics or a noticeable avoidance of certain subjects can be indicative of personal boundaries or concerns. This is where sensitivity and respect come into play, ensuring that communication doesn't wade into unwelcome waters. Conversely, openness and enthusiasm often manifest in messages that are thought-out and engage with the other person's inputs, showing genuine interest and attraction.

Sometimes, the most telling lines are the ones not written. Silence or ghosting can speak volumes, and understanding its underlying message can be vital for maintaining one's peace of mind in the tumultuous world of digital dating. It's important to learn not to second-guess every silence but to recognize patterns and consistent behaviors, anchoring interpretations in genuine instincts rather than assumptions driven by insecurity.

Mastering the ability to read between the lines doesn't happen overnight. It requires practice, reflection, and most importantly, feedback from real interactions, both online and offline. As trust and understanding grow between two people, the necessity to overanalyze diminishes, replaced by a genuine appreciation of the unspoken connections that have formed. Each successful interpretation strengthens the relationship, fostering a sense of closeness and mutual understanding.

Ultimately, reading between the lines enriches digital interactions, translating text into stories and emoticons into emotions. It bridges the gap between raw data and human connection, ensuring that our digital dalliances remain deeply human. This skill turns the guessing game of online communication into an art form, adding depth to relationships as old as communication itself, carried forward into the pixelated world with a tender grace. Navigating these nuances can redefine one's approach to online dating, transforming it from a daunting landscape to an exciting canvas of possibilities.

Digital Do's and Don'ts

In the ever-expanding universe of online dating, a set of unwritten rules can make the difference between a meaningful connection and a digital faux pas. As we dive into the world of online flirting and etiquette, let's explore the digital do's and don'ts that will guide you toward genuine interactions and avoiding potential missteps.

First and foremost, let's talk about timing.

Patience is a virtue often tested in the rapid pace of digital communication. While we're all accustomed to the instant gratification that a ping from our smartphones brings, the incessant demand for immediate responses can be overwhelming. It's essential not to mistake silence for disinterest or unavailability. Life happens outside the virtual realm, and sometimes delays are unavoidable. When you wait, you inject a sense of thoughtfulness into your interactions. Taking time allows for carefully constructed responses that align with your true intentions rather than reactive, spur-of-the-moment replies.

However, this patience is not a free pass to ghosting. Maintaining consistency in communication fosters an environment where interest is clearly demonstrated, and intentions are understood. While there is no predefined duration that dictates when a conversation should flourish, the golden rule is simple: consistency breeds clarity. Leaving someone hanging without an explanation is akin to closing a book just as the plot thickens. Ensure you communicate openly about your time constraints or lack of availability to respond swiftly.

Just as important as timing is the tone of your digital interactions. In the absence of vocal intonations and non-verbal cues, text can be a breeding ground for misunderstandings. Sarcasm, while it may add a touch of humor in face-to-face interactions, can easily be misconstrued in text form. Always evaluate your audience; what might work for one person might not necessarily land well with another. Emojis and well-placed punctuation can help clarify your tone, but don't over-rely on them—authenticity is still your best tool.

Let's not forget the importance of respect. This seems like an obvious do, but in the vast and varied worlds of online dating platforms, it's often the little things that are most easily forgotten. Respect means valuing the other person's time, emotions, and boundaries. Remember that behind every profile is a real person with their own stories, experiences, and expectations. Kindness and empathy go a long way in creating a space where genuine connections can develop.

Part of showing respect is choosing your words wisely. The anonymity of the internet might tempt some to express unchecked thoughts and emotions, but the consequences of digital speech are real and lasting. What you say in the heat of the moment could leave lasting impressions that aren't easily forgotten. Before pressing send, consider whether your words contribute to a positive and engaging conversation or whether they might be better left unsaid.

As we talk about words, it's crucial that your words are your own. Unfortunately, the digital realm offers plenty of opportunities to borrow phrases and 'perfect' messages from others online. Authenticity should be your guide. Reciting lines you didn't craft diminishes the sincerity of your interactions. Trust in your ability to present the best version of yourself, showing vulnerability and honesty in your effort to forge real connections.

Another key element in effective online communication is proper photo etiquette. Your profile picture is usually the first impression you make. Ensure it reflects a true representation of who you are, showing both your personality and interests in a tasteful way. Avoid overly edited pictures or photos that could be misleading. Be proud of who you are and let that authenticity shine through—alluring not through filters, but through being genuine.

Conversely, respect others' personal space and boundaries by keeping your photography requests respectful and within norms of decorum. Remember, nobody is obligated to share anything they are not comfortable with. Building trust takes time, and respecting someone's comfort level is paramount in laying that trustworthy foundation.

Avoid the temptation to put potential matches in a lineup, sending the same generic messages indiscriminately. Instead, take the time to personalize your correspondence, showing that you've paid attention to profile details. This thoughtful approach not only makes you stand out but fosters a sense of being seen and appreciated. People are more likely to engage positively when they feel you've made an effort to understand them beyond what their profile picture displays.

While digital platforms bring the advantage of accessibility, remember to keep your expectations realistic. Just because you have the ability to connect with someone instantly doesn't guarantee immediate compatibility or mutual feelings. Building chemistry online can take time. Be patient, and don't rush the process. Allow your interaction to unfold naturally; it's an art guided more by intuition than algorithmic suggestions.

Respecting privacy takes precedence over fear of missing potential connections. Never press for more information than someone is willing to give, and respect their privacy while maintaining your own guard until trust is securely established. This digital exchange becomes a dance of balancing openness with protecting personal boundaries; striking this balance seamlessly builds a foundation upon which genuine relationships can grow.

It's tempting to project your life's highlights in interactions but strive also to keep things realistic and relatable. Presenting an idealized version might momentarily impress, but the long-term rewards come from being relatable and true to yourself rather than creating a persona that you think others will prefer. Transparency encourages trust, a crucial element in transforming digital claims into real-world experiences.

Lastly, it's essential to know when to take things offline. The world of online flirting is thrilling, offering ample opportunities for exploration. But sooner or later, translating virtual flirtations to real-life interactions should be considered. When both parties indicate eagerness to meet in person, plan something low-pressure, ensuring both feel comfortable and safe for that crossover experience.

People often worry about making mistakes, but remember, navigation is about learning and iterating over time. In the grand tapestry of connection, missteps are just parts of a larger design. Through mindful interactions, you continue contributing to a broader narrative focused on inclusivity, empathy, and deeper understanding.

When navigating the digital world of dating, empathy, patience, authenticity, and respect are your greatest allies. Equipped with these tools, you're not only following online etiquette but forging paths toward meaningful and sustainable relationships that transcend mere digital flirtations.

Chapter 7:
Overcoming Dating App Anxiety

As we delve deeper into the world of digital dating, it's normal to feel a knot of anxiety when confronting the flashy realm of swipes and hearts. The notion of reducing one's personality to a series of pictures and brief descriptions can be daunting, causing even the boldest among us to fret. But it doesn't have to be this way, and overcoming this anxiety starts with embracing authenticity and stepping into the digital space with confidence. You'll find that by focusing on genuine interactions, rather than the overwhelming abundance of profiles, the experience morphs into one less about expectation and more about exploration. Remember, the goal isn't merely to be seen, but to connect with someone who resonates with your true self. For the shy user hesitant to dive in, small steps can pave the way: starting conversations with kindness, setting realistic goals, and trusting in the process. It's all about building confidence online, not through pretense, but through understanding that there are others just like you—hopeful, eager, and ready to find something meaningful amidst the digital cacophony.

Strategies for the Shy User

Embarking on the journey of digital dating can be daunting, especially for those who consider themselves shy or introverted. While the idea of swiping through countless profiles might feel liberating to some, for the shy user, it can be overwhelming. Yet, in this vast digital realm, there are numerous strategies to help shy individuals find their space and voice.

First, embrace your nature. Understand that shyness isn't a flaw but part of who you are. It can shape meaningful interactions, as those who take the time to know you may appreciate the depth of your thoughts and the strength of your character. Start by creating a profile that highlights your interests and hobbies rather than focusing excessively on self-promotion. This can attract like-minded people, allowing conversations to flow more naturally around shared interests.

Strategically approaching interaction is another important method. Begin with platforms that offer more than just a quick swipe feature. Apps that focus on more detailed profiles and meaningful matches can provide a comfortable space for shy users to express themselves. Features like prompts or question-based matches can guide the conversation without putting all the pressure of starting a dialogue on you.

Once your profile is set, practice makes perfect. Engage in low-pressure interactions to build confidence. You might start by commenting on shared interests or asking questions that show you're genuinely interested in getting to know the other person. Remember, initial messages don't have to be grand gestures of wit and charisma; sometimes, a simple, authentic hello with an open-ended question can work wonders for sparking a conversation.

Building a support system is equally essential. Share your experiences with friends or family members who are supportive and understanding of your personality. They can offer valuable feedback or encouragement, providing a boost of confidence. Moreover, witnessing their dating experiences can sometimes give insights and strategies you hadn't considered.

During the messaging phase, take advantage of the natural pauses in online conversation. Unlike face-to-face interactions, digital conversations don't require immediate responses, giving you time to think about what you want to say. Use this to your advantage to express yourself authentically.

Set intentions before logging on. Affirmations can be beneficial in reminding yourself that it's not about changing who you are but about letting the right person appreciate your uniqueness. You might say, "I am open to genuine connections and will stay true to myself," or "I allow myself to be vulnerable and open to new possibilities." These intentions can help ground you and prevent the anxiety of interaction from becoming overwhelming.

Another effective approach is carving out time for reflection. After engaging in conversations, take a moment to reflect on what felt comfortable and what didn't. Understanding patterns in your comfort levels can help you steer future interactions in a way that feels genuine and manageable. It's not just about learning what to say but discovering what makes you feel secure and authentic.

Don't be afraid to set boundaries too. While it's crucial to challenge yourself to step out of your comfort zone, it's equally vital to know when to step back. If a platform or interaction doesn't resonate with you, it's okay to take a break or switch to another that suits your style better. This ensures dating remains a positive, enriching experience rather than a stressful endeavor.

Additionally, embracing creative communication can be a game-changer. If words aren't always your forte, consider expressing interest through humorous GIFs, song recommendations, or by sharing an intriguing article. These can act as conversation starters and show your personality uniquely. Articulating thoughts doesn't have to be limited to typing out long messages—there are multiple avenues to express interest and resonate with someone across digital platforms.

Finally, shy users can benefit from engaging in self-love and personal growth outside the digital sphere. Engaging in activities that nurture confidence and self-awareness can indirectly bolster your online dating life. Whether it's joining a book club, taking up a hobby, or practicing mindfulness, such activities can enhance your self-esteem and provide interesting topics to discuss when conversations pick up online.

So, for those who thrive in quieter environments, know that digital dating doesn't mean you need to shout to be heard. It's about finding the right volume for your voice and learning how to tune into the frequencies of those who appreciate the nuances of your character. Embrace your shyness as an ally rather than an obstacle—and remember, the goal isn't to change who you are. Instead, it's about discovering who you're comfortable being when connecting with others, both online and off.

Building Confidence Online

In the realm of dating apps, confidence is the invisible thread that can weave connections stronger than the most artfully constructed profile. It's the missing ingredient that often leaves us hesitating before hitting "send" on a message or double-guessing the sincerity of a match. Building confidence online is not about creating a facade; it's about embracing authenticity and letting your true self shine through the digital screen.

Starting with the basics is crucial. Imagine yourself on a stage, the spotlight on you, but in the comfort of your own space. You don't need to perform; you need to communicate your genuine self. This begins with a strong sense of self-awareness. Knowing your strengths and embracing areas for growth provides a solid foundation to interact with others genuinely.

An essential step in this journey is crafting a profile that reflects who you really are—quirks, passions, and all. Being open and honest in your profile sets the right tone. It filters out potential matches who might not be on the same wavelength, saving you from unnecessary stress. Fotos showcasing your hobbies or places that hold meaning to you say more than words ever could, inviting comments and fostering shared interests.

Messaging a match for the first time can feel like standing on the edge of a high dive. The anxiety of making a perfect impression can be overwhelming. But confidence is built through action. When you initiate a conversation, focus on authenticity over perfection. Ask engaging questions and give thoughtful answers, seeing each interaction as a chance to learn rather than to impress. This shift in perspective transforms apprehension into an opportunity for connection.

Another powerful tool for building confidence is practicing self-compassion. The digital world is fast and, at times, ruthless. Rejections, ghosting, or mismatches are inevitable. However, reframing these situations as part of the process rather than personal failures can ease the sting. Each interaction, successful or not, offers insights and learning experiences. Be gentle with yourself; growth takes time.

Consider the people you admire in your life—those who navigate the world with poise. Often, their confidence stems not from how others perceive them but from a deep-seated assurance in who they are. In the digital dating landscape, anchoring your self-worth internally rather than externally is crucial. Affirmations can be a simple yet effective method to cultivate a positive mindset. Repeating statements like "I am worthy of love" or "I am confident in my interactions" reinforces beliefs that impact behavior.

Participating in online communities or forums focused on shared interests can also bolster your confidence. These spaces allow interaction without the pressure of romantic expectations. Engaging in conversations about things you are passionate about not only builds your communication skills but also reminds you of your core strengths and values, which can naturally enhance your online dating profile.

Let's not forget the role of humor in easing anxiety and building confidence. A well-timed joke or lighthearted comment can break the ice and showcase your personality. Humor invites others to feel comfortable and connected, dissolving barriers that often arise from the perceived need for perfection.

Equally important is the support network you build outside of the dating app world. Friends and family who uplift and support you can offer perspective and encouragement when online dating challenges arise. They can remind you of your value, cheer your victories, and provide a safe space to process setbacks.

As with any journey, patience is key. Confidence doesn't blossom overnight but rather grows with each meaningful interaction and insightful reflection. Setting realistic expectations and recognizing that everyone is on their own journey can help maintain a balanced perspective.

In the end, building confidence online is about embracing vulnerability and authenticity. It's about understanding that you bring something unique to the table and that your worth is not dictated by matches or messages. With each step forward, each message sent, or each photo update, you're not just navigating the digital dating world—you're mastering it in your own unique, confident way.

As technology continues to blur the lines between virtual and real-world interactions, the skills you hone through online dating—clarity in communication, resilience in facing rejections, and authentic self-expression—become invaluable assets. They empower you to navigate the complexities of modern romance, whether online or offline, with confidence and grace.

Chapter 8:
Safety and Privacy in the Digital Age

In today's fast-paced digital dating world, ensuring your safety and protecting your privacy are as essential as making a good first impression. As we swipe and message our way through potential connections, the need to safeguard personal information becomes paramount. With the rise of online scams and cyber threats, knowing how to recognize suspicious activity is crucial. Embrace anonymity by sharing details judiciously and keeping sensitive data under wraps. By harnessing the power of technology, not just for connection but for protection, you empower yourself to enjoy the digital dating journey confidently. Trust your instincts and leverage security features offered by dating platforms—your heart and your data deserve it.

Protecting Personal Information

In today's digital dating world, protecting personal information has never been more crucial. As technology evolves, so does the sophistication of data theft. When you dive into the realm of online dating, you're not just putting your heart out there; you're also exposing personal data. Being casual about your data can make you vulnerable to risks, ranging from identity theft to financial scams. Thus, it's essential to be proactive and vigilant about the information you share, and where you share it.

Dating apps are designed to connect people, but they also collect substantial data to function effectively. This can include your location, habits, preferences, and even financial information if you opt for paid features. Understanding what data is collected and how it can be used is the first step toward safeguarding your privacy. It's worth reviewing the privacy policies of any app you use, as tedious as that might seem. These documents can reveal who has access to your data and how it's protected—or not.

The digital footprint left behind on dating platforms can also paint a detailed picture of who you are. Inadvertently, this footprint might include identifying details you didn't intend to share. Always be cautious about integrating social media accounts with dating profiles. This might make logging in easier, but it also links various parts of your online presence, multiplying privacy risks. It's a good idea to use a separate email address solely for dating apps to help compartmentalize your online activities.

When creating a dating profile, less can often be more. Opt for sharing general information that highlights your personality without divulging specific personal details. For instance, mentioning a love for hiking won't compromise your safety like sharing the exact trail you hit every Saturday morning might. Ponder every entry you make—is it revealing something that could be misused?

One might think it's harmless to share snippets of personal life to build rapport early on. However, the reality is that the digital realm can be deceiving. Until trust is established, avoid sharing details like your home address or workplace location. Consider using virtual phone numbers for communication to maintain an extra layer of privacy.

Taking control of your profile settings is a powerful yet underutilized step in protecting personal information. Many users don't realize they can adjust who sees their profiles and what information is publicly available. Some platforms allow you to remain hidden unless you choose to connect with another user, thereby minimizing exposure.

Encryption and secure connections are pivotal in protecting your exchanges on dating platforms. Ensure the apps and websites you interact with have solid security protocols in place. Look for platforms that use end-to-end encryption, so only you and the person you're communicating with can read your messages.

Phishing scams and catfishing are perennial threats in online dating, aiming to exploit unsuspecting users. Always approach new connections with a healthy level of skepticism until you're confident they're genuine. Keep an eye out for inconsistencies in stories or any push for financial transactions, which are often telltale signs of fraud. Never share bank details or engage in money transfers, no matter how trustworthy someone might seem.

When meeting someone for the first time offline, even more precautions are necessary. Stick to public places and let a trusted friend know your whereabouts. An additional safety measure is arranging your own transportation, ensuring you have the means to leave if needed. Remember, maintaining personal security is a continuous practice that shouldn't be relaxed even after meeting people in person.

Some may fear that imposing too many privacy measures will dampen the spontaneity cherished in romance. However, being wary doesn't mean being closed-off. It's about creating a safe space for genuine connection to flourish. When both parties are mindful of privacy, it fosters trust and shows respect—an attractive quality in any potential partner.

Today's dating landscape demands smart navigation through both romantic and technical terrains. By being informed and cautious, you're not just protecting data; you're prioritizing well-being and paving the way for authentic relationships. Empower yourself with knowledge and take control of your personal information with every swipe or message you send. The essence of romance remains unchanged, but in this digital age, a little caution goes a long way.

Ultimately, protecting personal information is about finding balance. It's about opening your heart, while keeping your data close. Each precautionary step you take is another foundation stone for a connection built on trust rather than fear. Foster a sense of digital security and peace of mind, allowing you to genuinely experience the joy and excitement of finding love online.

Recognizing and Avoiding Scams

In the digital age, where the pursuit of love can start with a simple swipe, the excitement of making a new connection often comes with risks. The romantic landscape is teeming with potential partners, yet it also harbors those who prey upon the emotionally and financially vulnerable. Learning to recognize and avoid scams in online dating is crucial for protecting both your heart and personal information. It's a journey of becoming not just a savvy dater, but a wise one.

Scams in the world of digital dating can take many forms, from identity theft to emotional manipulation. One of the most common tactics used by scammers is catfishing, where they create a fake online persona to entice their targets. Often, these profiles seem too good to be true, projecting an aura of perfection that can lure unsuspecting individuals into a web of deceit. Recognizing the signs of a catfish is the first step in safeguarding yourself. Watch out for inconsistencies in their stories, reluctance to meet in person, and refusal to engage in video calls. If they dodge these interactions, consider it a red flag.

Financial scams are another prevalent threat in the online dating scene. These scams might start with genuine-seeming conversations, slowly building trust before hitting you with a sob story or an urgent financial need. They might claim to be stuck overseas without funds or have a sudden medical emergency that requires immediate cash. Protecting your financial well-being begins with never sending money to someone you haven't met in person. No matter how dire their situation seems, remember that true love doesn't come with a price tag.

The evolution of technology has also brought about more sophisticated scams, including those that involve malware and phishing attempts. Scammers might share links that, when clicked, install malicious software on your device designed to steal your personal information. To counteract this, ensure you have comprehensive antivirus and anti-malware protection on your devices and exercise caution before clicking on any links sent by someone you just met online. Trust your instincts—if something seems off, it probably is.

Behavioral cues can also be telltale signs of a scam. Pay attention to overly extravagant claims of love or grand promises made too quickly. Real, meaningful connections usually develop gradually and don't skip over getting to know each other's genuine selves. If someone appears too eager to declare their undying love or press for more intimate details even before meeting, it might be a tactic to manipulate you emotionally.

The rise of romance scams isn't just a problem for older generations; young people navigating the lanes of digital romance are also at risk. As digital natives, the younger crowd often feels confident in their judgment, but scammers are continually refining their tactics to keep up with tech-savvy individuals. Education on how to avoid these pitfalls is an ongoing process that everyone should engage in. Being aware of common scam setups can arm you with the knowledge needed to avoid falling victim.

One of the most empowering tools you can use is verification. Many dating platforms offer features that allow users to verify their profiles through various methods. Take advantage of these security measures. Verified profiles typically display a badge or checkmark, reducing the likelihood of encountering a scammer. Additionally, use reverse image searches on profile pictures to ensure the person you're speaking with isn't using someone else's photos.

Privacy settings on dating platforms and social media can serve as a first line of defense. By controlling the amount of personal information you share online, you're reducing the chances of scammers accessing sensitive details they could use against you. Be selective with the details you disclose and regularly review your privacy settings to ensure they align with your comfort level.

Let's shift focus to a key aspect of preventing scams: open communication with trusted friends or family. Sharing your online dating experiences with people you trust can provide an outside perspective that might catch red flags you've overlooked. They can offer support and advice if something doesn't seem right, helping you remain grounded in situations that might cloud your judgment.

Report suspicious behavior to the dating platform immediately. Most platforms have dedicated teams to review and handle reports of scams, working to remove fraudulent profiles and protect other users. By reporting, you're not only helping yourself but contributing to a safer community for everyone.

It's vital to remember that scamming isn't a reflection of your intelligence; it's designed to exploit human emotions, something everyone possesses. Awareness is your most potent defense. Stay informed about the latest scam tactics and take preemptive steps to protect your online interactions. While the digital world offers incredible opportunities for connection, it's imperative to navigate it with caution, vigilance, and self-awareness.

Ultimately, the goal of recognizing and avoiding scams isn't just about self-preservation. It's about ensuring that your quest for love remains a joyful and enriching experience. By embracing best practices in digital safety, you're paving the way for genuine connections to flourish. In a world where technology aims to bring us closer, let's ensure that integrity and authenticity guide our path.

Chapter 9:
Transitioning from Online to Offline

Embarking on the journey from digital flirtations to real-world encounters is a thrilling turning point in modern romance. As you stand on the cusp of this transition, the anticipation can be both exciting and nerve-wracking. Success in translating a virtual connection into a meaningful in-person meeting requires a delicate blend of confidence and authenticity. It's about embracing vulnerability and allowing your online persona to seamlessly merge with the real you, creating a space where genuine connections can flourish. Planning your first date with care, considering a setting that encourages easy conversation, can set the stage for a memorable impression. As the digital veil lifts, the essence of what connected you online reveals itself more vividly in shared smiles and direct eye contact. This pivotal moment isn't just about relocating where you talk—it's the exhilarating start of discovering deeper layers of compatibility, feeling the chemistry in the air, and turning a promising digital thread into a potential love story woven with real experiences.

Planning the First Date

The first date represents a critical milestone in the journey of transitioning from online to offline. It's where the pixels on the screen meet the tangible atmosphere of face-to-face interaction. While digital exchanges may build interest and chemistry, there's nothing quite like the alchemy of real-world encounters. Planning this initial meeting is both an art and a science, requiring thoughtful consideration to ensure that burgeoning connections can flow seamlessly from virtual to visceral.

One of the first elements to consider is the choice of location. This decision is pivotal, as it sets the tone for the entire encounter. While conventional wisdom might suggest a dinner, it's worth exploring unique settings that invite comfort and conversation. A cozy coffee shop or a scenic park walk offers the intimacy to engage in meaningful dialogue without the distractions of a glamorous venue. Think about places that align with mutual interests shared during online chats, as this can bring your conversations to life.

Timing is another factor that can't be overlooked. Choosing a time that aligns with both your schedules can prevent unnecessary stress. Weekends can offer a lazy afternoon backdrop, but mid-week evenings can feel equally endearing if managed correctly. It's essential that both parties feel relaxed and not rushed. Time matters less than the energy and enthusiasm you both bring to this new chapter.

Make sure you communicate openly about expectations for the first date. The excitement of firsts can sometimes lead to assumptions that aren't aligned. When expectations are clear, the day feels more intentional and both parties can focus on simply getting to know each other better. Is the meeting strictly casual or is there a romantic intention behind this in-person meet-up? Open communication before the date can help in setting the appropriate expectations and reduce the chances of misinterpretation.

The art of conversation plays a crucial role in transitioning from online interactions to face-to-face dialogues. Think of subjects that can bridge your digital exchanges with real-world discussions. The best conversations are those filled with curiosity and openness. Listen as much as you share. This dynamic not only respects the pace of dialogue between two people but also reveals how comfortable both feel in each other's physical presence.

As for the date's activities, keeping things light and engaging can help ease any nervousness or pressure. Choose something interactive that allows for shared experiences or mutual discovery. Whether it's visiting an art exhibit or trying out a cooking class together, these activities transcend the traditional and encourage collaboration. This sense of sharing creates a new narrative unique to both of you and can act as a foundation for future dates, if all goes well.

It's important to remember that authenticity is your greatest asset. Being yourself—quirks and all—lays the groundwork for genuine connections. Pretenses can create barriers that prevent true intimacy from developing. Embrace your moments of vulnerability, for they open the door to deeper understanding. This is as much about seeing how your personalities mesh as it is about creating impressions.

Even though the aim is to cultivate a meaningful connection, keeping things light-hearted and fun remains important. Laughter is a beautiful language that strengthens bonds quickly. It makes the date memorable and enjoyable, countering any awkwardness that might sneak in. But also don't shy away from silences; sometimes they provide the comfortable space for introspective appreciation.

Also, don't underestimate the power of spontaneity during the date. While plans are a strong backbone, allowing for spontaneous decisions can lead to delightful surprises. This improvisation dynamically changes the course of the date into something memorable. Walking by a street musician and stopping for a few moments to enjoy the melody, or deciding to try a new dish on the menu—all these add flavors to your shared experience.

After your first date, reflecting on the experience can provide clarity. Was there a sense of ease? Did your conversations flow as effortlessly in person as they did online? These reflections can guide your next steps, helping you decide whether there is potential for a deeper connection or if you should part as acquaintances who simply enjoyed a shared moment in time.

Should both parties feel mutual excitement to plan a second date, it's always nice to express it. A simple follow-up message thanking each other for the company and expressing your thoughts about the meeting can build on the foundation laid down during the date. This outreach strengthens the transition between just getting to know one another and entering the realms of companionship.

In summary, planning the first date is a beautiful blend of practicality and spontaneity, sprinkled with moments that can invigorate the hearts involved. Dive into this experience with an open heart and an adventurous spirit, allowing yourself to be surprised by the authenticity of human connection beyond the veil of screens.

Making a Memorable Impression

Transitioning from the digital realm to the tangible world offers a unique mix of excitement and nervousness. As screens have become our modern-day windows to the world of romance, the shift to face-to-face interaction can feel like stepping onto a stage. The spotlight now shines on you, offering a chance to reveal your genuine self and make an indelible mark on your date's memory. This pivotal moment is your opportunity to transform virtual chemistry into real-life enchantment.

First impressions matter immensely, as they often set the tone for what might follow. The magic lies in the details—those small, conscious choices that convey respect, genuine interest, and authenticity. Perhaps it starts with a warm, genuine smile that evokes comfort, or the choice of a meeting spot that shows consideration and an understanding of shared interests. Such gestures speak volumes, reflecting who you are and how much you value the other person.

Consider your attire, for instance. It's an expression of your personality and how you wish to be perceived. While there's no one-size-fits-all approach, dressing in a way that makes you feel comfortable and confident can enhance your presence. It's not about fitting into a mold, but rather embracing your individuality while showing you've put thought into the occasion. Mix this personal touch with subtle elements that align with your date's preferences, if known, and you create a bridge of empathy right from the start.

As the conversation unfolds, active listening becomes crucial. It's more than just hearing words; it's about understanding the sentiments behind them. Responding with thoughtful questions or reflections demonstrates that the person across the table matters. This act of listening nurtures a space where genuine connection can bloom, free from the disruptions of digital distractions.

Remember, it's not just about sharing your stories. Equally important is creating an environment where your date feels comfortable sharing theirs. Encouraging openness and being attentive to verbal and non-verbal cues makes the interaction enriching for both parties. Seek to discover stories, experiences, and perspectives that differ from your own, adding layers of depth to the developing connection. Contrasts invite curiosity, and curiosity can lead to a beautiful dance of discovery.

Body language doesn't lie. It's the unspoken word that complements what you say. Maintaining eye contact, for example, signals interest and sincerity, creating an intimate connection beyond mere words. A gentle nod while listening or an occasional smile can enhance your verbal exchanges, allowing emotions to flow naturally. Striking the right balance in your use of body language can transform a simple conversation into a memorable rendezvous.

Humor, when used wisely, can lighten the mood and foster an immediate bond. A shared laugh lays the foundation for a joyous time and might even flatten any initial awkwardness. However, it's crucial to be sensitive with humor—what one finds amusing, another might find off-putting. Pay attention to your date's reactions, and let that guide your repartee.

Shared activities can be a wonderful icebreaker, redirecting attention from the pressure of conversation to the joys of a shared experience. Whether it's visiting an art gallery, attending a concert, or simply taking a walk in the park, the activity sets a natural scene for interaction. Engaging in something both of you enjoy cultivates a feeling of camaraderie and creates shared memories to reminisce about in the future.

One often underestimated aspect of making a memorable impression is expressing gratitude. A simple "thank you for today" at the end of the meeting encapsulates appreciation for the time spent together and opens the door for future engagements. Acts of gratitude exude warmth and humility, reinforcing the bond that started with a message and blossomed into a more profound connection.

As you navigate the transition from online to offline interactions, remember that authenticity will always shine through. Being true to yourself while respecting the journey of discovery that dating embodies is key to leaving a lasting impression. The stories you share and the moments you create together form the initial chapter of what could be a much larger narrative.

Ultimately, making a memorable impression isn't about being perfect. It's about being present and genuine—celebrating both commonalities and differences with openness and curiosity. Such authenticity not only enhances the potential for a deeper connection but also enriches your own experience within the modern dating landscape. By respecting the uniqueness of the offline date and embracing its potential, you lay the groundwork for genuine and fulfilling connections beyond the digital puppetry.

Chapter 10:
Long-Distance Love in a
Connected World

In our ever-connected world, long-distance love challenges and rewards those daring enough to embrace it. Technology has crafted an intricate tapestry of possibilities, turning the daunting miles into mere numbers. Picture this: oceans apart, yet sharing breakfast via video call, or texting each "goodnight" as if lying side by side. While these digital tools bridge distances and nurture intimacy, they demand creativity and commitment to keep the spark alive. Relationships that thrive on the electronic pulse find ways to balance virtual and real, weaving in moments of surprise, shared playlists, and virtual date nights. It's the synergy of hearts and screens that fuels a unique modern romance, reminding us that love, when kindled with intention, knows no borders.

Keeping the Spark Alive

In a world that's more connected than ever, maintaining the flame of a long-distance relationship requires creativity, dedication, and a sprinkle of magic—the kind that stems from intention and genuine emotion. It's more than just bridging the geographical gap; it's about fostering an emotional closeness that defies physical separation. The digital landscape offers an abundance of tools and opportunities to help keep the spark alive, but like any flame, it needs consistent tending to flourish.

Communication is the lifeline of any relationship, yet for those separated by miles, it's paramount. Scheduled calls or spontaneous video chats, whatever your style, can quickly become intimate rituals that give rhythm to your days. Hearing a loved one's voice or seeing their face, even through a screen, can turn ordinary evenings into cherished moments. It's as simple as syncing your schedules to watch a movie together or virtually attending a concert; shared experiences, even from afar, strengthen bonds and create new stories.

Routine can be the enemy of romance, so injecting unpredictability keeps things thrilling. Surprise messages hidden in a favorite novel, unexpected postcards, or even a playlist created just for them can serve as delightful reminders of your connection. These gestures, grand or small, spark joy and help bridge emotional distances.

Commit to learning something new together. Engaging in mutual interests fosters deeper intellectual and emotional connections. Whether it's learning a language, appreciating fine wines, or mastering the art of yoga, shared passions can make conversations richer and increase your anticipation for the next time you'll be physically together.

Long-distance love isn't just about enduring the days apart; it's about celebrating the relationship itself. Celebrate milestones, no matter how small—a first meeting, the first month, or simply surviving another workweek apart. A shared calendar may remind you to mark these moments, but personalizing your celebrations makes them more meaningful. It's texting an affectionate message to say how proud you are of one another or sending a surprise delivery of their favorite snack.

Romantic gestures have evolved with technology; now, a thoughtful meme, a witty GIF, or a romantic song link can say what words sometimes can't. It's in these seemingly trivial exchanges that modern love finds its way to maintain warmth and humor. Romantic love letters are alive and well, even if they're in the form of emojis dancing across cellphone screens.

It's crucial to handle misunderstandings with care, especially when technology can amplify them. Distance can make conflict resolution tricky, but viewing disagreements as opportunities for growth makes every challenge worth it. Practicing patience and empathy goes a long way. Addressing concerns openly and honestly solidifies trust, which is the bedrock of any relationship.

Planning future visits is not just about logistics; it's about anticipation and shared dreams. Whether it's a weekend getaway or cozy nights in, having something to look forward to can ease the ache of separation. As you map out your itinerary, the anticipation builds like a tangible thread connecting your love even when you're apart.

The saying "out of sight, out of mind" doesn't hold water with modern modalities of staying connected, but setting a vision for the future does. Dream together. Who do you want to be as a couple? Discuss these dreams and desires candidly. These discussions can energize the relationship and provide direction, helping to navigate the complexities of distance with purpose.

Of course, always keep room for spontaneity. Long-distance relationships might thrive on planning and scheduling, but leaving room for spur-of-the-moment interactions kindles excitement. Unexpectedly FaceTiming just to share something special that happened in your day, or a next-flight-out surprise to show up at their doorstep, infuses your love story with spontaneity and thrill.

Finally, cherish the journey rather than just the destination. Every connection, in texts, calls, or visits, weaves the fabric of your unique relationship. It's these shared moments, dotted with laughter, understanding, and patience, that define your partnership. So don't just look forward; revel in the now.

Long-distance love in our connected world isn't about surviving the separation; it's about thriving in it. Behind every message ping and virtual touch lies the belief that love transcends boundaries. With every technological advantage at our disposal, the art of keeping the spark alive lies in pairing them with authentic emotions and intentional actions—and in doing so, crafting an enduring love story that knows no distance.

Technology's Role in Bridging Distances

We exist in a time where technology's power to connect is unparalleled, reshaping how we experience romance across miles. The notion of long-distance love once meant enduring lengthy separations and scarce communication, punctuated by the occasional phone call or handwritten letter. Today, digital innovations transform these relationships, blurring the lines between physical presence and virtual interaction.

Platforms like video calls and instant messaging apps bring loved ones face-to-face, no longer bound by the constraints of geography. These tools create a new kind of closeness, a digital intimacy that's becoming more significant and meaningful. When longing and loneliness threaten, a quick video chat or shared meme can bridge the gap, transforming what it means to be "apart."

Despite these innovations, maintaining romance in a long-distance relationship presents challenges. It requires conscious effort, a willingness to be vulnerable, and a commitment to staying emotionally intertwined. Balancing these elements can be delicate, but technology offers unique tools that help partners maintain the warmth and familiarity of their bond.

Virtual reality, for instance, is pushing boundaries further, enabling partners to share experiences in new ways. Though still emerging, virtual environments allow couples to attend concerts, explore cities, or even share a home-cooked meal together. Technology's development hints at a future where digital spaces become extensions of our own lives, bridging emotional distances like never before.

Consider the role of shared digital experiences beyond visual interaction. Music playlists curated together, collaborative Pinterest boards, or even shared calendars become vessels of connection. These digital touchpoints are unique to our era, building a life that, while played out on screen, feels incredibly real and personal.

Yet, there's an art to leveraging technology without losing sight of the authentic, emotive power underlying every interaction. It's about finding balance and ensuring that the tools amplify the relationship rather than replace genuine human interaction. The goal is not to substitute presence with pixels but to craft new pathways of sharing, understanding, and caring.

The power of surprise and anticipation plays a crucial role in long-distance love. Technology facilitates spontaneous "I love you" text messages or unexpected voice notes. Such gestures remind us of the small, yet profound, acts that sustain relationships, letting partners feel cherished and valued despite the miles.

Moreover, technology provides innovative ways to create shared rituals, maintaining connection through daily routines. Couples might start their mornings together over a video call, sharing breakfasts from different time zones. Or they might wind down their evenings with a bedtime story read aloud, preserving intimacy and closeness. These digital rituals forge bonds that are just as meaningful as their physical counterparts.

Of course, such an evolution in connection wouldn't be possible without the ingenuity of developers and their continuous pursuance of better, more immersive technologies. As artificial intelligence and machine learning evolve, anticipating our needs and preferences, they promise to further personalize and enhance long-distance interactions.

The ability to send thoughtful digital recognitions through AI-powered reminders, or even predictive algorithms suggesting what might brighten a partner's day, enriches the relational experience. It's about using technology to anticipate needs, not replace genuine concern and understanding.

At its heart, technology in long-distance love serves as an enhancer, a facilitator of communication that overcomes the once-impossible barriers of time and space. It provides endless possibilities for maintaining and nurturing relationships, helping couples remain attuned to each other, constantly exploring new ways to express their love.

It's important, however, to approach this digital world with mindfulness. The danger lies in letting technology become an intermediary rather than an enabler. Authentic connections rely on the emotional threads that hold us together—threads that technology can reinforce but never should entirely weave.

Finally, as we embrace technology's presence in our romantic endeavors, we must also pursue sincerity, ensuring that all digital interactions reflect our truest selves. Whether journeying through the terrain of long-distance love or simply nurturing a close relationship in our immediate environment, technology is not merely a tool but a companion in crafting the shared stories of our lives.

In this ever-evolving world, we can't underestimate the potential technology carries in bridging distances. As digital intimacy shapes modern relationships, it continues to redefine notions of proximity and presence, making what was once far away feel remarkably near.

Chapter 11:
The Role of Social Media in
Modern Relationships

Social media has become a significant force in modern relationships, weaving its web through every interaction and connection. In a world where moments are captured and shared instantly, social platforms have shifted the landscape of intimacy and communication, offering both new opportunities and challenges. From sharing milestone moments to navigating the complexities of public versus private lives, partners find themselves balancing the desire for virtual validation with the need for personal connection. Establishing boundaries becomes crucial in this digital arena, where expectations often blur between individual identity and shared experiences. As couples negotiate these online spaces, they also explore how digital intimacy can enhance, rather than replace, genuine emotional bonds, fostering a deeper understanding of themselves and each other in a hyper-connected world. Balancing these dynamics is not just about managing digital impressions but nurturing the authenticity that underpins romantic connection in this ever-evolving landscape.

Defining Boundaries and Expectations

In the intricacies of modern relationships, defining boundaries and expectations is a cornerstone of healthy engagement. With social media weaving itself deeply into our daily lives, it inevitably becomes a backdrop for our interactions, especially romantic ones. However, integrating these digital landscapes requires careful navigation to ensure they enhance rather than detract from our intimate connections.

Boundaries serve as the framework within which relationships can thrive. In the context of social media, this often relates to what parts of your relationship are shared publicly and which remain private. Each couple must have candid conversations about their comfort levels regarding posting personal moments online. While one partner might feel at ease sharing everything, the other might prefer keeping certain experiences intimate. To avoid misunderstandings, it's crucial to discuss and agree on these boundaries early on.

Expectations in relationships set the stage for how partners interact and what they anticipate from each other. Social media has added a new dimension to these expectations—messages that are seemingly left on 'read', likes on someone else's photos, or the frequency of public interactions can all stir insecurity if expectations aren't well-defined. Open communication is essential in clarifying what social media behavior is acceptable and what crosses the line, ensuring both feel valued and understood.

When social media becomes part of the relationship's landscape, it can feel like you're constantly on display. Each post and interaction can be scrutinized by friends, family, and exes. This visibility can lead to pressure to present a perfect relationship, which is often far from reality. By setting boundaries, couples can protect their relationship from becoming an unwelcome public spectacle, allowing them to focus on authentic growth away from the public eye.

Balancing the personal and the public calls for mutual respect and understanding. Deciding whether to engage in public declarations of love or to remain subtle online—especially in the early stages—often requires compromise. Is it important for your significant other to be 'Facebook official', or does that notion feel trivial to you?

Understanding each other's perspectives helps negate potential disputes arising from mismatched expectations.

The digital age amplifies the speed at which relationships progress, sometimes skipping foundational stages. Clear boundaries can counteract this, ensuring that the couple moves mutually rather than being swept along by the tide of expectation set by social media norms. Being intentional about time spent offline together might do wonders for deepening connections, allowing for genuine understanding and companionship to flourish.

It's not uncommon for past romantic interactions to become ghostly figures hovering over current relationships via mutual connections or old posts. Boundaries can help mitigate the impact of the digital presence of your or your partner's past. Discussing how much of your past you want in your present is vital to avoid unnecessary scars from reopening.

Social media's constant connectivity can lead to a sense of never truly being alone or away from the relationship. Establishing a digital detox or agreeing on device-free times can be liberating. In creating these pockets of time, couples can engage deeply without the constant pinging interruptions that technology brings.

Trust plays a pivotal role when setting boundaries and expectations. Building and maintaining trust through transparency allows both partners to feel secure, with or without social media. It's about ensuring that digital interactions don't supersede personal ones—that an online persona doesn't overshadow genuine interaction.

Remember that boundaries aren't static; they evolve alongside the relationship. Regular check-ins about what works or what doesn't ensure that both partners remain on the same page. This evolution is natural and a sign of maturation in relationships.

While technology offers exciting avenues for interaction, it's crucial not to lose sight of the fundamental human elements that make relationships rich and rewarding. Listening, showing empathy, and being present are behaviors that transcend any digital interface. By focusing on these, couples can ensure that their interactions online complement, rather than complicate, their experience of love.

Managing Digital Intimacy

In our increasingly digital world, managing intimacy has taken on new layers and complexities that were inconceivable decades ago. Digital intimacy asks us to consider how technology restructures our intimate interactions and redefines our boundaries. It's not just about safeguarding privacy; it's about nurturing closeness through screens while maintaining healthy personal space. Navigating this landscape requires keen awareness and thoughtful negotiation of our digital behaviors and expectations.

At its core, digital intimacy is an evolving dance of proximity and distance, where people find themselves sharing deepest thoughts through text or video, yet feeling a physical absence. Surprisingly, digital platforms can foster remarkable intimacy. Think about those late-night conversations held through glowing screens, where words typed out carry as much weight as those whispered in person. Yet, it's accompanied by the risk of confusion and misinterpretation, challenges traditional relationships might never encounter.

Social media platforms, with their promise of constant connection, can sometimes blur the lines between online interaction and invasive overexposure. Lovers showcase their lives together, weaving narratives through shared posts and tagged photos. While these digital stories might appear seamless, the reality is frequently more nuanced. One has to be vigilant about what parts of one's relationship to spotlight and what to keep in sacred trust. Balancing openness with privacy can be tricky but necessary to maintain a relationship's sanctity.

With digital intimacy, there's a new realm of expectations around availability and responsiveness. Timing and frequency of communication can signal interest levels, but overemphasis on real-time replies could mask genuine engagement with routine interactions. It's about finding a pace that respects both partners' commitments while still fostering a sense of togetherness.

Recognizing digital body language is a crucial skill in managing digital intimacy. What's left unsaid or uncommented upon in an online interaction can mean as much as spoken declarations. A lack of response may not always denote disinterest—it might be an invitation to deeper discussion offline, a signal to pivot to other modes of communication that foster richer interaction.

It's also essential to address the impact of virtual personas on relationships. Curating an online presence can inadvertently create a distorted version of reality. This crafting of one's image may impact a partner's perception, sometimes sparking unnecessary jealousy or discontent. Being mindful of authenticity in digital interactions can avert misconceptions and reinforce trust.

Within long-term relationships, digital intimacy plays a different role. Here, it can offer a canvas for keeping the romance alive. Digital gestures, whether they be sweet texts in the middle of the day or sharing a playlist that conjures memories, can act as gentle reminders of affection and attention. They're small acts that nurture bonds, especially when partners find themselves physically apart due to life's demands.

In comparison, new relationships might ride the digital wave differently. For such connections, initial communications might revolve around gauging compatibility. Here, digital intimacy serves as both a realm of discovery and a testbed for chemistry. Are we comfortable discussing our quirks and interests, and how do we handle zone differences in text-heavy conversations? These factors can be pivotal in determining if a fledgling relationship stands the test of time.

We can't ignore the challenges accompanying digital intimacy. Online misunderstandings can escalate quickly, potentially tainting a budding relationship. Recognizing when an issue is too significant to handle via a messaging app and redirecting the conversation face-to-face—or voice-to-voice—can prevent escalation. Establishing boundaries around when and how to engage digitally is vital. Sometimes, a digital pause is necessary to re-center emotions and focus on what's most important.

Managing digital intimacy also means being wary of the permanence of online content. What gets shared in a moment of vulnerability could become fodder for future conflicts if not handled with care. Establishing early on what's private, what's public, and what remains within the sacred realm of a partnership protects both parties involved.

Another aspect of managing digital intimacy involves negotiating shared virtual spaces. The digital age has democratized access to information, but when it comes to relationships, sharing passwords or maintaining joint accounts demands delicate handling. Does being intertwined digitally make you a stronger entity, or does it invite unnecessary scrutiny into minutiae of each other's lives? Diverse answers to these questions exist, each tailored to the unique relationship it serves.

As with many aspects in life, the key to managing digital intimacy resides in communication. Constant, clear dialogue ensures both partners understand and respect each other's needs and boundaries. It's about having those frank conversations about how intimate interactions online reflect—or deviate from—the relationship dynamic that exists in the physical world.

The essence of digital intimacy is adaptability. As technology continues to evolve, so will the ways it influences our personal connections. Navigating these shifts demands openness to adaptation and an enduring commitment to learning. It's all about evolving with your partner, letting technology enhance your journey without dictating it.

Ultimately, managing digital intimacy becomes a tapestry woven from mutual understanding, respect, and strategic sharing. It's about crafting an environment where digital tools enhance love and connections rather than overshadow them. Embracing the opportunities these virtually intimate spaces offer, while maintaining a grounding in what's real and meaningful, paves the way for richer, fulfilling relationships in the digital age.

Chapter 12:
The Influence of Algorithms on Love

In the modern landscape of digital dating, algorithms quietly shape and steer the currents of romance as we know it. These unseen forces compile and process significant amounts of data, matching potential partners with an intricate blend of precision and unpredictability. Despite their promise, there's a hidden complexity to these digital matchmakers, often influenced by biases embedded within the code, affecting our chance at connection and sometimes narrowing our world instead of broadening it. As you navigate these algorithm-led paths, it's crucial to ponder their impact not only on who's presented to you but also on how personal preferences and societal expectations are shaped. Understanding these subtleties can empower you to use technology as a tool in your quest for genuine, heartfelt connections, remaining vigilant against the influence of hidden biases while maintaining the authenticity of your romantic aspirations.

How Data Shapes Your Matches

In the digital age, love isn't just a matter of the heart; it's also a matter rooted in algorithms and data science. The very matches you examine on your dating app screens aren't born out of haphazard chance. Instead, they're crafted through a sophisticated dance of numbers, preferences, and predictive modeling, orchestrating who you may—or may not—meet.

Your romantic journey begins with a stretch of data collection. Every swipe, heart, and X signifies a choice that feeds into an algorithm's calculations. Have a penchant for creatives? Prefer partners who share your love for culinary delights? Your choices and preferences inform these algorithms, hinting at hidden desires that you might not even be consciously aware of. Algorithms take all these data points and start shaping the potential matches brought to your digital doorstep.

The sheer volume of data processed can be staggering. Imagine the weight of billions of swipes, the thousands of bios crafted with care and humor, the candid yet calculated profile pictures. This is the realm where algorithms thrive, sifting through the noise to understand what makes each user tick. And it's not just about the matches you've liked; it's also about the ones you've decidedly not liked. Each dismissal is an insight, a pixel in the broader portrait of your dating profile that algorithms assemble.

Despite the data's role in shaping your matches, there remains an air of unpredictability, a touch of fate in its own digital form. Algorithms aren't flawless; they're informed by the humanity behind the data. They attempt to replicate the serendipity of meeting someone at a coffee shop or at a mutual friend's gathering. Yet, they often stand on a razor's edge—balancing between your stated preferences and your untapped potential interests, urging you to widen your horizon.

But how does this sea of data translate into a meaningful interaction, or better yet, lasting love? Consider the nuanced predictions made about your cultural interests, lifestyle choices, and even the frequency of your app usage. Each factor is accounted for and used to narrow the options to those most aligned with your life and its rhythm. These algorithms strive to match you with someone whose digital signature echoes your own, fostering compatibility and chemistry that might blossom offline.

This data-driven matchmaking serves as both a map and a mirror. It guides you through potential connections but also reflects back insights into your own behavioral patterns. Perhaps you're drawn more to humor than previously thought or someone's profile whose understated nature appeals to a nuance you cherish. This reflection encourages introspection, enabling a deeper understanding of what—beyond the surface—actually matters to you in a partner.

Yet, relying heavily on algorithms has its pitfalls. The profiles shown could inadvertently create a false sense of homogeneity. The algorithm seeks patterns, and left unchecked, it could funnel you towards matches that mirror past choices rather than challenge you to explore something new. Users often fall into the trap of echo chambers, where their digital interests reverberate loudly at the cost of encountering enriching diversity.

This leads to the conundrum of algorithmic bias. Though programmed with unbiased intent, these algorithms can inherit developmental or systemic biases. How they process race, gender, or orientation might influence not only match recommendations but also perpetuate stereotypes. It's essential to address these biases and push for transparency, ensuring that these digital matchmakers remain fair and inclusive.

Nonetheless, there is room for optimism. Platforms are increasingly aware of these biases and strive to refine their algorithms, ensuring matches reflect values of diversity and representation. Enhanced user control—encouraging feedback on matches and interaction preferences—can create a more tailored and genuine dating experience. This degree of control not only empowers choice but also promotes authenticity.

In a world where the search for love often feels overwhelmed by infinite possibilities, algorithms serve an essential purpose as gatekeepers. They sort out the chaos, present options, and facilitate connections that might otherwise remain undiscovered. While data shapes your matches, it is ultimately the human touch, the shared laughter, the small gestures, that turns a digital introduction into a heartfelt connection.

Beyond the technical scaffolding of ones and zeroes, lies the age-old quest for partnership and companionship. Algorithms serve to ease and enhance this journey, removing some of the friction found in conventional encounters. While they may pave the path, the journey—and the destination—remain authentically human.

Understanding Algorithmic Bias

In our quest for love in the digital age, algorithms stand as unseen matchmakers, wielding incredible power over our romantic destinies. Yet, these technological arbiters are far from impartial. Understanding algorithmic bias is critical as it holds sway over who we meet and potentially fall in love with. It's a dense tapestry of code, data, and human input that shapes the digital dating landscape in ways we're often blissfully unaware of.

Algorithmic bias occurs when computer algorithms systematically favor certain outcomes based on skewed or prejudiced data. This bias isn't exclusive to dating apps; it manifests in myriad systems we interact with daily. In the realm of online dating, this bias can translate into some users' profiles being highlighted while others remain in the shadows. It's not a mere technological glitch but a reflection of societal biases seeped into the code.

To grasp how algorithms can be biased, one must first understand their building blocks: data. Dating apps rely heavily on user data to function. They collect and analyze everything from your age, likes, and dislikes to the length of time you linger on a particular profile. Yet, this data is influenced by human behaviors and prejudices and can introduce bias. Suppose a community predominantly prefers certain racial or cultural attributes, consciously or unconsciously. In that case, the algorithm learns and amplifies these biases rather than challenging them.

Think about the potential impact: profiles of individuals from marginalized backgrounds might receive fewer matches, potentially reinforcing existing social inequities. Even if you don't actively discriminate, the algorithm might do it for you, suggesting matches within a narrow segment it perceives as your type. While these systems aim to make connections more efficient, they inadvertently perpetuate biases that exist in the real world.

Furthermore, bias in algorithms can arise not only from data but from the developers themselves. Humans design algorithms, and despite the best intentions, they might encode their biases into these systems unintentionally. These biases can reflect developers' personal preferences or assumptions about what is "normal" or desirable, leading to an imbalance in match suggestions and interactions.

So, what does this mean for someone trying to forge meaningful connections in the ether of online dating? Awareness is the first step. Recognizing that what you see on your screen is shaped by algorithms—and those algorithms may have blind spots—allows you to approach your digital interactions with a critical eye. It's important to understand that the endless parade of profiles crafted by an algorithmic hand isn't random; it's a result of collected data and input that could inherently carry certain prejudices.

Reflect on your experience within these apps. Have you noticed how you might see similar profiles repeatedly, or how certain profiles rarely pop up in your feed? Ask yourself: Are the people you're not seeing more a reflection of algorithmic predispositions than personal preferences? This reflection can encourage a shift from passive swiping to conscious engagement, prompting users to question their own preferences and biases.

Addressing algorithmic bias in dating isn't just about personal introspection, though; it's also about calling for transparency and accountability from companies that develop these apps. Users should demand more information about how these algorithms are designed and how decisions are made. Initiatives for more inclusive datasets and bias checks in algorithm design are crucial steps toward leveling the playing field and ensuring everyone's profile has an equitable chance of being viewed and appreciated.

Moreover, some dating platforms are increasingly leaning into machine learning techniques that actively adjust for bias. These advancements are promising, offering hope that as technology evolves, it can become more inclusive and reflective of the diversity within human experiences and attractions. However, it's crucial to remember that technology is not a silver bullet. Human understanding, empathy, and intent must accompany it to create a truly fair dating environment.

Empowering users with insights about algorithmic bias fosters a more mindful approach to digital dating. It emphasizes the need for continual learning and adaptability, prompting individuals to question not just how they use these platforms but how these platforms use them. It's about reclaiming agency and not letting a string of code define the possibilities for love and connection.

In conclusion, understanding algorithmic bias in digital dating apps is about peeling back the layers of technology to reveal the human elements underneath—elements that are subject to flaws like any other aspect of human society. This awareness is not just about improving individual user experiences but about contributing to a broader dialogue on equality and fairness in all digital interactions. As we navigate this new frontier of love, let's do so with open eyes and an informed heart, ready to challenge and change the technology-driven narratives around romantic connections.

Chapter 13:
Balancing Technology and Authenticity

In an age where technology often dictates the pace of our lives, maintaining authenticity in romantic connections has become both an art and a necessity. While digital platforms provide the convenience of meeting people beyond our immediate social circles, they can also foster superficial interactions that lack depth. The challenge lies in navigating this digital realm without losing sight of the genuine connections we seek. Cultivating authenticity means peeling back the veneer of curated profiles and spotlighting true intentions. It's about being brave enough to show your true self, embracing vulnerability, and encouraging others to do the same. Both courage and clarity can help us break the cycle of fleeting encounters, and foster relationships filled with meaning and authenticity. By combining our digital tools with an honest pursuit of connection, we can navigate the dating landscape with a sense of purpose that transcends mere swipes and clicks.

Avoiding the Trap of Superficial Connections

In a world driven by technology, we often find ourselves swiping through potential partners as if we're browsing an online catalog. While such convenience is unparalleled, this rapid approach can lead to connections that remain only skin-deep. Superficial connections may offer instant gratification, but they often lack the substance needed for long-term fulfillment and romantic growth. Technology's role in facilitating these quick matches is undeniable, yet we must delve deeper to understand the importance of authenticity in our virtual interactions.

The allure of superficial connections begins with the fear of vulnerability. Opening up to someone, especially a stranger met online, can seem daunting. Technology allows for a layer of protection—profiles are curated, messages are premeditated, and real-time reactions are buffered by screens. While this mode offers a sense of safety, it also encourages a facade that can prevent genuine connection. Moving beyond these barriers involves embracing vulnerability over perfection, revealing your true self rather than an idealized version.

One of the key challenges with superficial connections is that they rarely satisfy our deeper emotional needs. Humans crave connection on multiple levels: emotional, intellectual, physical, and even spiritual. Superficial interactions often solely focus on physical attraction or shared interests, ignoring the complexities of our inner lives. If we limit ourselves to these surface-level engagements, we risk missing out on the profound joy that comes from truly knowing and understanding another person.

To avoid this trap, it helps to be intentional and mindful in your engagements. Take time to ask questions that go beyond typical icebreakers. Instead of merely exchanging likes and dislikes or discussing current trends, delve into topics that reflect core values and life perspectives. Conversations centered around personal growth, aspirations, and even setbacks can unveil layers of a person's identity, laying the groundwork for a deeper connection.

Moreover, it's crucial to bring authenticity to your online persona. While it's tempting to showcase only the most dazzling aspects of your life, authenticity breeds connection. Sharing moments of vulnerability or imperfection doesn't make you less attractive; it makes you real. In a world brimming with filters and staged photographs, honesty is a breath of fresh air. When people can glimpse beyond the surface, they're more likely to feel a genuine bond.

Authenticity doesn't stop at profiles and messages. When you're transitioning from online to real-life interactions, consistency is key. Maintaining the same openness and honesty in person as you did online helps solidify trust, an essential component in any meaningful relationship. This approach can pave the way for a more seamless transition from virtual romance to reality, reducing the awkwardness that sometimes accompanies first meetings.

Creating a balanced approach to dating in the digital age involves both introspection and intentionality. Reflect on what you truly seek in a relationship and question whether your current connections support that vision. Are you engaging with others in ways that foster depth, or are you settling for the immediate rush of superficial exchanges? This kind of self-awareness can guide you toward more meaningful interactions and ultimately more fulfilling connections.

Additionally, don't underestimate the power of taking breaks from the digital world. With time away from screens, you have the chance to reconvene with your inner world and cultivate self-awareness, a vital element in forming authentic relationships. When you understand yourself better, the connections you form are less likely to be superficial. This reflective practice enables you to return to the digital sphere with a renewed sense of purpose and clarity.

Finally, it's essential to set boundaries that nurture deeper connections. In a sea of potential matches, it's easy to stretch yourself thin, chatting with multiple people without really investing in any one relationship. Prioritize quality over quantity. Focusing your energy on a few promising connections allows for richer dialogues, leading to stronger, more authentic bonds. Establishing these priorities can help sidestep the transient nature of superficial engagements.

The journey toward avoiding superficial connections in technology-driven dating is not without its challenges. However, with conscious effort and an openness to vulnerability, the digital world can still be a landscape where genuine love blooms. It requires introspection, honesty, and intentionality, but the rewards—a deeper understanding of and connection with another person—are undeniably worth the endeavor.

The Importance of Being Genuine

In a world awash with digital interactions, the quest for authenticity has never been more imperative. As we navigate the landscape of technology-driven romance, being genuine offers a compass to guide our connections. Amidst the allure of algorithms and the seduction of curated profiles, maintaining authenticity in our interactions has become a revolutionary act. It challenges the default mode of presenting polished versions of ourselves and invites substance over superficiality.

Authenticity resonates because it's grounded in truth. When you communicate authentically, you invite others to see you for who you really are, quirks and all. This vulnerability builds a foundation for genuine connections. The digital sphere, for all its innovations, still demands the age-old recipe of trust, sincerity, and openness. These qualities encourage deeper conversations, fostering bonds that transcend the screen. In essence, being genuine is about cutting through the noise and finding a melody that both participants can tune into.

The idea of being genuine isn't just an expectation for others; it's a personal commitment. It requires introspection and a clear understanding of your values, desires, and boundaries. This self-awareness not only aids in personal growth but also ensures that the connections formed are meaningful and rooted in reality. By engaging in honest self-reflection, you're better equipped to offer a real version of yourself, making the dating experience more enriching and less transactional.

While technology aids connection, it also can fog our view of what's real. Filters, both literal and metaphorical, blur the lines of authenticity. In dating apps, where first impressions are often gleaned from photos and brief bios, there's pressure to present an enhanced persona. But authenticity breaks through this facade. By being genuine in your profile and interactions, you send a powerful message that you're seeking something real. This honesty can be a magnet for those who are also yearning for depth and sincerity in their interactions.

Furthermore, authenticity breeds resilience in relationships. When both parties show up as their true selves, they lay the groundwork for trust and understanding. Conflicts are inevitable, but they're navigated with greater compassion and empathy when everyone's cards are already on the table. Pretenses fall away, leaving space for real dialogue and compromise. Being genuine offers the stability to weather the ups and downs inherent in any relationship, nurturing growth rather than erosion.

However, it's crucial to navigate the fine balance between being genuine and oversharing. Authenticity doesn't mean unloading every facet of your life upon first meeting. It's about being honest and open while respecting your own boundaries and those of others. It's perfectly okay to hold back until trust and comfort pave the way for deeper disclosure. True authenticity evolves with time, growing as familiarity and connection deepen.

The journey to authenticity isn't devoid of challenges. Social pressures often push the narrative of fitting into certain molds, especially in the realm of dating. Societal norms, beauty standards, and expectations can obscure our genuine selves. Yet, breaking free from these constraints can be liberating. Embracing who you are and courageously sharing that truth in your dating life teaches others to do the same. It's a ripple effect that can lead to a more inclusive and accepting dating culture.

In the dance of digital dating, authenticity acts as a grounding partner—one that steadies the steps in an otherwise choreographed performance. It's about pausing amidst the swiping frenzy, taking a deep breath, and asking what you truly want. It's about choosing conversations that matter over countless matches. It's about prioritizing meaningful interactions that align with your core values over fleeting engagements that only offer surface-level satisfaction.

Ultimately, the significance of being genuine comes down to one fundamental truth: love is not a transaction. In a world so focused on swipes, likes, and algorithms, it's easy to forget that the tenderness, warmth, and connection offered by authentic relationships is irreplaceable. When you allow your authentic self to shine, you create opportunities for encounters that bring joy, growth, and genuine companionship.

As technology continually evolves, the need for authenticity becomes even more pronounced. Each digital interaction offers a chance to show up in a way that's aligned with who you are. By weaving genuineness through the fabric of our online interactions, we can transform the current dating paradigm into something that enriches lives rather than detracts from them. In doing so, we can foster a dating landscape ripe with potential for genuine, lasting love.

The truth is, authenticity is the thread that binds us to one another in meaningful ways. It's the foundation upon which lasting love stories are built. As you navigate the digital dating world, let the courage to be genuine be your guiding star, illuminating the path towards fulfilling and authentic connections. After all, there is immeasurable beauty in the ordinary moments shared when two genuine hearts connect amidst the vast digital landscape.

Chapter 14:
Finding Love Beyond the Apps

As the glow of smartphones and the allure of dating apps relentlessly command our attention, it's all too easy to forget the myriad ways love can surprise us when we step away from the screens. Let's explore the realm where serendipity lingers, in moments and places where digital dating doesn't reach. Picture a chance meeting at a local art gallery, or a shared laugh at a community event—spaces rich with possibilities for those willing to open their hearts and minds. Beyond algorithms and curated profiles lies a world brimming with authentic experiences waiting to be embraced. By engaging in activities we're passionate about and nurturing friendships, we create a fertile ground where genuine connections can blossom. In rediscovering traditional avenues of love—through social clubs, volunteer work, or simply striking up a conversation in a café—we cultivate encounters that are refreshingly real, reminding us that sometimes, the best kind of love can't be swiped or typed, but felt deeply and unexpectedly.

Alternative Ways to Meet People

In an age dominated by digital connections, it's easy to forget that there are countless ways to meet people outside the confines of a screen. While dating apps have certainly changed the landscape of finding love, they are not the only avenue. Embracing more traditional or alternative methods can inject a refreshing authenticity into one's search for connection. For many, relinquishing the endless scroll of profiles leads to more enriching encounters and narratives that begin in the most unexpected moments.

Consider community involvement as a rich ground for meeting new people. Joining clubs, participating in local events, or volunteering allows like-minded individuals to unite over shared interests and values. These activities not only provide an opportunity to meet new people but also present the chance to engage in meaningful work. The bonds formed over mutual passions often create a strong foundation for lasting relationships, as they are rooted in genuine understanding and shared experiences rather than curated digital personas.

Another avenue ripe with potential is found in the professional realm. Networking events or industry-specific meetups can sometimes spark unexpected romantic connections. These settings encourage individuals to present their best selves, driven by professional courtesy and shared professional interests. Collaborating on projects or bouncing ideas off one another can lead to chemistry that transcends job titles. The professional confidence that emerges in these environments can foster attraction and lay down honest ground for more personal connections.

Then there's the captivating world of shared hobbies and pursuits. Whether it's a cooking class, a dance workshop, or a hiking group, engaging in activities that promise enjoyment and fulfillment can often bring people together. In these settings, individuals are more apt to be genuine, as they're engaged in something they love. This authenticity often leads to more meaningful connections because the mask of societal expectation is often put aside in favor of pursuing joy. Plus, nothing acts as a better ice-breaker than shared enthusiasm for a common interest.

Connecting through mutual friends can also be a comfortable and natural way to meet new people. Friends often play the role of matchmaker, either intentionally or unintentionally, when they introduce you to their extended circles. These connections carry an added layer of trust, as they come with the implicit endorsement of a friend. This social circle mix-and-match often occurs at gatherings such as weddings, house parties, or even casual get-togethers, where the relaxed atmosphere encourages open interaction.

Immersive travel experiences offer another unconventional method to meet potential partners. Traveling opens us up to new cultures and perspectives, often broadening our horizons in the process. It has an unparalleled ability to strip away pretenses and foster impromptu friendships, as travelers are usually in search of authentic experiences. Whether bonding with fellow travelers over the shared wonder of a new city or connecting with locals who offer insider insight, the connections made while traveling can be both deep and unexpected.

Creative pursuits and artistic environments can also serve as fertile grounds for connection. Art galleries, music events, theater performances, and writing workshops gather individuals who are in touch with their creativity and emotions. Engaging with someone's art or creative expression can lead to profound insights about their personality and values. These interactions stimulate the mind and appeal to the heart, making them ideal environments for encounters that go beyond superficial attraction.

Let's not ignore the allure of spontaneous social interactions that happen in everyday places. Coffee shops, bookstores, and even public transportation become the unlikely backdrops for some of the greatest love stories. These serendipitous moments remind us that opportunity waits just around the corner, when we least expect it. Sometimes, all it takes is a simple smile or a mutual acknowledgment of an interesting book to strike up an engaging conversation.

Ultimately, stepping outside the digital world to meet potential partners requires bravery and a willingness to embrace vulnerability. However, the rewards of forging connections in these alternative settings often outweigh the comforts and confines of app-based dating. In a world where algorithms rule many aspects of our lives, actively choosing to engage with the world around us can feel both liberating and enriching. By diversifying our approaches to connection, we increase our chances of finding love in places we never thought to look, teaching us that sometimes true connections are best sought in the simplicity of human interaction.

Rediscovering Traditional Methods

In a world dominated by screens and swipes, it's easy to forget about the subtler, age-old methods of finding connection. Many people yearn for something tangible, a romance not dictated by algorithms but sparked in the warmth of a genuine moment. As alluring as modern technology can be, there's undeniable magic in the traditional ways of meeting someone. These methods, though timeless, are often overshadowed by the fast-paced digital options.

Meeting someone through a shared activity or interest can create a bond deeper than many digital introductions. Joining clubs or groups, such as a local sports league, book club, or dance class, opens opportunities for organic encounters. Sharing passions not only brings about potential romantic connections but also fosters friendships that can lead to unexpected introductions. There's an authenticity to glancing across the room to meet someone's eye, a spark that's different from a carefully curated profile picture.

Then there's the serendipity of places we frequent, like cozy cafes, bustling markets, or vibrant community events. These are places where chance encounters lead to conversations, laughter, and perhaps the beginning of something more. People who frequent the same spaces might have more in common than they initially realize, creating a fertile ground for connection. This kind of interaction relies on genuine curiosity and the willingness to let ourselves be open to the randomness of life.

Rediscovering traditional methods also means relying on the network of friends and family. While it can feel vulnerable to open up about our desires for connection, those close to us often know us well, sometimes better than we know ourselves. From casual setups to planned gatherings, trusted people in our lives can introduce us to potential partners who align with our values and interests. It's a method of matchmaking that predates digital algorithms yet remains remarkably effective.

Social gatherings, weddings, and parties offer ideal opportunities to meet people outside of our usual circles. They're places where people are often more relaxed and open, ready to engage in conversation. Amidst the music and laughter, genuine connections can form. These events provide a backdrop for spontaneity, a chance for authentic interactions without the pressure of digital impressions.

Consider the art of letter writing, a slower-paced method of communication that encourages thoughtfulness and depth. While emails and messages are convenient, writing a letter requires slowing down and contemplating what we truly want to convey. In an age of immediacy, there's profound romance in waiting for a letter to arrive, in anticipating the words carefully chosen by someone who dedicates time to engage beyond fleeting text exchanges.

Even traditional blind dates have their merits, allowing for a meeting without preconceptions formed by digital footprints. These encounters can be a refreshing change, grounded in the potentially enigmatic nature of discovering someone. The experience of meeting a person with fresh eyes, based purely on another's recommendation, forces us to be present and attentive in the moment.

Nostalgia, too, plays a role in the revival of traditional methods. Many are drawn to simplicity, longing for connections similar to those of previous generations. The tales of how grandparents met, often devoid of technology's influence, resonate with people who desire the same unembellished reality—a reminder that sometimes stepping away from tech can lead to fulfilling experiences.

With the resurgence of community-focused activities, like volunteering or attending local arts performances, new avenues for connection emerge. Involvement in communal efforts not only nurtures personal growth but also brings like-minded individuals together, reinforcing bonds through shared dedication to a cause. Again, it's about leading with shared values and experiences rather than initial physical attraction or curated profiles.

There's an element of mindfulness and authenticity required when we rediscover these traditional methods. They demand patience and an openness to the unexpected, qualities often overshadowed by the instant nature of modern dating. Embracing these methods is akin to investing in a slow-building narrative, rich with opportunities to discover and rediscover what it means to truly connect with someone.

This isn't about turning away from technology entirely, but integrating the best of both worlds. Imbuing our lives with both modern convenience and traditional warmth can create a holistic romantic experience. By acknowledging the charm and power of traditional methods, while navigating a digital landscape, we open ourselves to a world of possibilities far beyond what an app can offer.

Chapter 15:
Challenges of Modern Dating

In the digital age where options are seemingly endless, the quest for love often feels both liberating and overwhelming. The sheer breadth of choice can make it challenging to commit, as the allure of the next potential perfect match is just a swipe away. Navigating mixed signals in the world of emojis, texts, and instant messages requires a new kind of emotional literacy, where intentions can be as blurred as the lines between online and offline interactions. Yet, amidst these challenges lies an opportunity to redefine what genuine connection means to each of us. By understanding the pressures and embracing authenticity over the superficial, we can find clarity and purpose in our romantic pursuits. Whether it's the hope of lasting love or the excitement of newfound chemistry, modern dating holds the promise of profound connections, if only we dare to look beyond the screen and into someone's heart.

The Pressure of Choice

In the vast landscape of modern dating, one of the most intriguing dilemmas is the overwhelming array of choices. With a simple swipe, we're presented with countless potential partners, each accompanied by a glimpse into their curated lives via photos, profiles, and bios. On the surface, it seems like an opportunity to finally find that ideal connection. However, the constant influx of choices can be both liberating and paralyzing.

This phenomenon isn't just about abundance; it's about the anxiety that comes with it. Imagine standing in front of an endless buffet. Initially, the variety is exciting, but soon, the pressure sets in. How do you choose the best dish without knowing what the others taste like? In the context of dating, each person we encounter represents a potential future, a myriad of what-ifs. The fear of missing out on a better match can lead to perpetual indecision and dissatisfaction with the choices made.

In today's dating economy, options are endless, and that's where the paradox of choice becomes truly apparent. Barry Schwartz coined this term, suggesting that while more choices can indeed increase freedom and autonomy, they can also lead to higher anxiety and less satisfaction. This is deeply evident in dating, where users continuously swipe, liking dozens of profiles, maybe even chatting with a few, but making no real progress toward a lasting connection. The endless scroll for 'the one' starts consuming an inordinate amount of time and emotional energy.

One aspect we must consider is the illusion of perfection. Dating apps present us with endless profiles, each more polished and appealing than the last, creating unrealistic expectations. Over time, this can train us to seek mythical perfection, leaving us chasing unattainable standards we're not even sure we want. This relentless pursuit of an ideal partner can lead to disappointment when real-life interactions reveal the complexity of human nature, flaws and all.

Moreover, the digital dating realm exploits a fundamental human trait: curiosity. With each swipe, we're drawn into the possibilities of uncharted personalities and potential romances. The micro-dose of dopamine released in these explorations can become a form of addictive behavior, enticing us to revisit platforms with the hope of finding something—or someone—better. This cycle can hook users into a loop of perpetual searching, always yearning for the next connection, yet rarely fostering depth in existing ones.

The sheer volume of options can also impact the depth and quality of connections. Instead of investing in truly getting to know one person, many individuals feel the pressure to keep their options open. This mindset prevents deeper bonds from forming because there's always the next potential match in the background. This element of choice often undermines commitment, making meaningful relationships feel elusive.

However, it's not all doom and gloom. The pressure of choice can become manageable with the right mindset and strategies. By defining clear intentions and understanding personal desires, individuals can navigate these waters more effectively. It's essential to balance excitement for new possibilities with the dedication required for meaningful relationships. Prioritizing quality over quantity and being intentional in our interactions can significantly transform the dating experience.

So, how do we mitigate this choice overload? It starts with self-awareness. Recognizing what you genuinely seek in a partner and being realistic about those expectations can anchor your journey toward meaningful connections. Having a set of non-negotiable values or traits in a partner, while remaining open to different personalities, can guide more intentional choices, curbing the overwhelming nature of endless options.

Furthermore, embracing the imperfections in yourself and others can foster a more accepting approach to relationships. Understanding that no one is perfect allows you to progress past superficial app-based attractions and delve deeper into forming genuine connections. Accepting that every individual comes with their own set of strengths and weaknesses is essential in nurturing lasting relationships grounded in reality.

An essential step is also redefining success in the context of dating. Instead of viewing it as finding the perfect partner, discover success in the quality of connections we make, the experiences shared, and the growth achieved from each encounter. By reframing our focus, the dynamics of choice beautifully transform from paralysis to endless possibilities, enabling a sense of optimism and adventure.

In conclusion, the pressure of choice in modern dating could be seen as both a curse and a blessing. By reclaiming control over our desires and expectations and approaching dating with openness and intentionality, we overcome the superficial paralysis, opening ourselves up to the profound beauty of human connection. It becomes less about the pursuit of a perfect partner and more about the journey of self-discovery, acceptance, and understanding. It's this artful navigation of choice that brings a romantic sincerity back into the heart of modern dating.

Navigating Mixed Signals

In the ever-evolving world of modern dating, mixed signals are an inevitable part of the journey. The digital age has amplified the ways in which messages can be received, interpreted, and often, misconstrued. One moment you're basking in sweet nothings delivered through perfectly articulated texts; the next, you're questioning why it's been three days since you heard from them. The volatility of online interactions can leave you feeling like you're deciphering a complex code, where each emoticon or punctuation mark holds the key to understanding what someone truly means.

Mixed signals are not a new phenomenon in the realm of romance. Yet, the explosion of digital communication channels has magnified their presence and complexity. Consider the multifaceted nature of texting. A simple "Hey" could be laden with enthusiasm or just a casual check-in, depending on the sender's intent and the recipient's frame of mind. Add into the mix the varied ways people communicate on dating apps, via social media, or in video calls; it's no wonder dissonance frequently occurs.

The digital landscape lacks the nuances of face-to-face interaction, where nonverbal cues like tone and body language play a crucial role in communication. This absence often leads us to rely heavily on our interpretations, filling gaps with assumptions that may or may not align with reality. It's this dynamic that propels us into the realm of cognitive overload, creating unnecessary stress and self-doubt about how we should respond or react. The question then becomes: How can we navigate this digital maze without losing sight of genuine connection?

A vital strategy is to embrace open communication. It sounds simple, but expressing your thoughts and feelings clearly can cut through a significant portion of the confusion. Directness doesn't just clarify intentions; it also establishes a foundation of trust, signaling that transparent communication is valued. This approach encourages your partner to be more forthcoming about their own feelings, reducing the likelihood of misinterpretation.

Learning to read between the lines—or resist doing so—can also be crucial. Our brains are wired to look for patterns, sometimes creating meaning where none exists. It's important to recognize when you're projecting your fears or desires onto someone else's ambiguous message. Developing emotional intelligence and mindfulness can help you stay grounded, ensuring you respond to what is actually being said—not what you think is being said.

Remember, patience is an indispensable ally when navigating mixed signals in digital dating. Everyone processes feelings and relationships at their own pace. Sometimes, allowing space for the other person to articulate their feelings or intentions can yield clarity, fostering a more authentic connection. Jumping to conclusions can prematurely end what might have been a budding romance worth exploring.

If mixed signals become a persistent pattern, it might be time to assess compatibility. Consistency in behavior is often a key indicator of a partner's investment in the relationship. Repeated incidents of hot-and-cold behavior can signal emotional unavailability or incompatible communication styles. While it's natural to want to give the benefit of the doubt, recognizing when to walk away ensures you prioritize your emotional well-being.

Mixed signals don't always have malicious origins. More often, they stem from a place of uncertainty or fear. Society's pressure to constantly be clear about our intentions can sometimes trap us in indecision. People are often afraid of being vulnerable, leading them to test the waters with partial truths or vague expressions. Knowing this can help you approach these situations with empathy, understanding that not every mixed message is meant to mislead or harm.

Ultimately, navigating mixed signals in modern dating involves a balance of awareness, communication, and self-care. By being proactive in how you express yourself and interpret others, you can minimize misunderstandings. Establishing clear personal boundaries is equally important. Understand what you need from a relationship and don't be afraid to communicate those needs. This not only empowers you but also filters out those who might not be able to meet your expectations.

In crafting a love life that thrives amidst mixed signals, you're not just responding to the whims of online interactions; you're creating an intentional, fulfilling space where your authenticity invites the same from others. While the digital age may have reinvented the rules, the core principles of trust, empathy, and honesty remain steadfast. Embrace these, and you'll find your way through the labyrinth of modern romance with far more confidence and clarity.

Chapter 16:
Diversity and Inclusion in Digital Dating

As we journey deeper into the digital dating world, the importance of diversity and inclusion becomes ever more apparent. In a realm where algorithms dictate connection and swipes are the currency of introduction, acknowledging and embracing diverse perspectives can not only enrich the dating experience but also challenge norms. By celebrating the myriad of cultures, orientations, and identities, digital dating platforms have the potential to create spaces that are welcoming and equitable for all. Yet, the path isn't without obstacles; discrimination and bias can seep into algorithms and interactions alike, necessitating vigilance and advocacy. Users and platforms alike are called to foster environments where varied experiences aren't just acknowledged but are celebrated, helping us weave a tapestry of love that's as complex and colorful as the world we live in. Through conscious effort and open dialogues, digital dating can truly reflect the beauty of inclusivity, creating connections that are rooted in mutual respect and understanding.

Celebrating Different Perspectives

In the vibrant mosaic of digital dating, diversity and inclusion aren't just ideals to aspire to; they're realities that enrich and enliven the experience of seeking connection. Embracing different perspectives isn't just about acknowledging differences; it's about celebrating them.

It's about understanding that each person brings their own unique story, culture, and viewpoint to the table, transforming what could be a monotonous interplay of profiles into a rich tapestry of potential relationships.

Digital dating platforms today host an extensive array of individuals from all corners of the globe. With one swipe, you can connect with someone whose life experience and background might starkly contrast with your own. This exposure to different perspectives enriches our understanding of love and companionship in profound ways. It compels us to step out of our comfort zones and embrace the beautiful complexity that diverse identities offer. By doing so, we learn to appreciate not just where someone is from, but what cultural nuances and personal narratives they bring.

However, embracing diversity goes beyond just appreciating differences in ethnicity, race, or cultural background. It's about recognizing and valuing the wide spectrum of gender identities and sexual orientations that many feel empowered to express openly in the digital dating space. This inclusivity revolutionizes the traditional dating paradigm, making room for relationships that defy conventional norms and empowering individuals to love freely and authentically.

Today's digital dating landscape allows individuals to broaden their horizons and experience romantic connections they might never have considered within their own social or geographical circles. This intersection of diverse perspectives not only forges personal growth but also deepens empathy. By engaging with individuals from different walks of life, digital daters challenge their preconceived notions and become more open-minded. This understanding paves the way for more meaningful conversations and genuinely fulfilling connections.

It's crucial to approach this digital dating cornucopia with an open heart and mind. While differing viewpoints can sometimes lead to disagreements or misunderstandings, they can also offer invaluable lessons and provoke thoughtful introspection. In fact, it's through these differences that couples often discover surprising commonalities—a shared appreciation for the same book, a love of the same dish, or a mutual passion for advocacy.

Navigating this landscape requires a mutual willingness to learn and grow together. It's about asking questions and sharing stories, listening as much as we speak, and allowing ourselves to be influenced by someone else's reality. This mutual exchange can strengthen a connection beyond the superficial, fostering a partnership grounded in acceptance, respect, and admiration for what makes each of us unique.

Moreover, celebrating different perspectives in digital dating doesn't mean erasing our own identities. Instead, it's about awareness and integration. It's about finding what uniquely resonates with us while staying open to the unfamiliar and sometimes uncomfortable. This delicate balance can be profoundly enriching, making our digital dating journey not only a quest for love but an exploration of human diversity.

The ability to date across diverse perspectives is not without its challenges, however. At times, the collision of vastly different worlds can lead to friction. Yet, these moments can also be opportunities for deeper understanding and growth. It's crucial to approach such interactions with humility and a readiness to listen. The beauty of this digital era is that it equips us with the tools and platforms to befriend, understand, and appreciate others far removed from our own day-to-day lives.

In embracing diversity, digital platforms also have the responsibility to promote inclusivity actively. This means fostering an environment where everyone feels welcomed and celebrated. Dating apps are increasingly aware of the importance of representation and inclusivity, striving to create spaces that respect and celebrate the full spectrum of human experiences. This shift signifies promising progress—helping individuals feel seen, valued, and cherished in ways that transcend pixels on a screen.

At the heart of it all, celebrating different perspectives in digital dating is about acknowledging the vastness of human connection. It's about understanding that love is a universal language with countless dialects. Every two souls that meet, converse, and connect add their unique tones and rhythms to the symphony of romance. In a world where differences are often highlighted as divisive, digital dating offers a space where those very differences are the threads that weave us together.

This chapter acknowledges the immense opportunity and joy found in meeting the 'other'—a person whose words, actions, and feelings might initially seem foreign but ultimately offer an invitation to a world filled with possibilities. As we continue to navigate the avenues of digital dating, let us lean into the celebration of diversity, savor the knowledge it brings, and find beauty in the wide array of perspectives and experiences.

Addressing Discrimination Online

In the vibrant world of digital dating, diversity is a double-edged sword. On one hand, the myriad of platforms and users make it possible to engage with people from different walks of life, fostering unprecedented opportunities for global connections. On the other hand, this vast pool can also become a breeding ground for biases and discrimination. Addressing discrimination online isn't just about confronting individuals who hide behind the anonymity of screens; it's about challenging systemic biases ingrained in the algorithms that power these technologies.

Digital dating mirrors the societal structures within which it operates. When these platforms were created, they inherited our world's imperfections, including stereotypes and prejudices. These systems are sometimes set up to prioritize certain "desirable" traits, making some profiles more visible than others. A person's photo, name, or matching preferences can unintentionally become discriminated filters. This isn't just limited to race or ethnicity; it's a sprawling web that includes age, body type, religion, and more.

Addressing discrimination online requires concerted effort from both platforms and users. For tech companies, this means creating algorithms that are more inclusive, and constantly revising them to remove inherent biases. Developers need to be keenly aware of how data is collected and used, ensuring that everyone has a fair chance at love. A heart, after all, can't be quantified with data points alone.

As users, we have the power to challenge discriminatory behaviors by being conscious of our own biases. Reflecting on what we seek in a partner and asking ourselves if these preferences are influenced by stereotypes is a good starting point. Embracing diversity in dating isn't about lowering standards but widening perspectives. By making a conscious effort to explore beyond the familiar, we open ourselves to enriching experiences that broaden our views and redefine beauty in expansive ways.

The beauty of digital dating lies in its limitless potential. What once might have seemed like impossible matches—whether due to geographical distances or cultural differences—are now achievable. However, this potential is squandered if users are dismissed due to prejudices that belong to another era. It's crucial to remember that every profile embodies a person with a unique story and looking beyond initial prejudices gives us the opportunity to connect with these stories.

Education plays a significant role in combating online discrimination. Providing resources and tools for users to learn about cultural sensitivity, communication methods, and prejudice can empower individuals to make more informed choices. It's about naming biases and calling them out, whether it's subtle microaggressions or overt dismissals based on race or religion. With education comes the power to shift perspectives and promote a culture of inclusivity.

Additionally, platforms can implement mechanisms to report and address discrimination swiftly and effectively. Having a robust system in place not only protects users from harmful interactions but also signals a stand against inequality. Building a supportive community where everyone feels valued requires a zero-tolerance policy towards discrimination and a commitment to fostering positive interactions.

One inspiring approach has been the rise of niche dating apps designed for specific communities. They have carved out spaces where people with shared experiences or backgrounds can connect without fear of rejection solely based on their identity. While these platforms are not a panacea for discrimination, they provide vital refuge for those who have faced prejudice elsewhere, and in doing so, they celebrate diversity as strength.

It's also essential to have dialogues about representation within dating apps. Diversity should extend to the marketing campaigns and success stories featured by these platforms to ensure that users feel seen and included. When people see themselves reflected in the community, it fosters a sense of belonging, making them more likely to engage positively.

Ultimately, the aim is to transform the digital dating space into one where inclusivity reigns supreme. This is not a task that rests on individuals or algorithms alone; it is a collective effort. By embracing diversity, challenging our biases, and advocating for equality, we can create a dating culture that genuinely reflects the variety of the human experience, transforming dating apps from mere technological tools into powerful agents of social change.

In summary, addressing discrimination online isn't a one-time fix but an ongoing journey. It requires vigilance, empathy, and an unwavering commitment to creating a space where love can flourish free from bias. As we navigate through this digital age, let us aspire to a future where connections are based on the contents of our hearts rather than the trappings of our identities. Love, after all, transcends any boundaries society might impose, and in acknowledging this truth, we move closer to a more inclusive reality.

Chapter 17:
Mindful Dating Practices

In a world where swipes are swift and decisions even swifter, embracing mindfulness in dating can seem revolutionary. This chapter invites you to slow down and savor the moments in your dating journey, encouraging a deeper awareness of your emotions and those of your partner. By grounding yourself in the present, you can cultivate meaningful connections that transcend the screen's two-dimensional allure. Mindful dating isn't just about picking the "right" person; it's about nurturing emotional intelligence and tuning into the subtleties of human interaction. This approach not only enriches your experience but also elevates the quality of relationships you foster, turning potentially fleeting encounters into opportunities for genuine connection. Allow yourself to become more attuned to your instincts and discover the power of being genuinely present—even in a fast-paced, digital world.

Staying Present in a Fast-Paced World

In the whirling eddy of modern dating, it often feels like time speeds up. Each swipe, message, and profile browse can whisk us away, leaving us tumbleweeding through the endless possibilities of romantic connections. Our phones flicker with notifications that demand immediate attention, drawing us into parallel universes of communication that stretch our emotional bandwidth thin. It's easy, amid this swirl, to lose sight of the here and now.

Mindful dating practices invite us to slow down, to anchor ourselves in the present despite the world spinning ever faster. This isn't just about quieting the noise; it's about enhancing the symphony so we can actually hear the music. In the realm of the heart, mindfulness acts as both a compass and a steady hand, guiding us through the fog of fast-paced interactions to meaningful connections.

Consider the act of waiting for a text back. We've all been there—hovering over our phones like suspenseful watchmen. But what if, instead, we shifted focus inward while embracing the moment's slow churn? Engage in activities that empower this transition from waiting to presence. Practice a simple breathing exercise or immerse yourself in an engaging task. Letting go of the compulsion to check messages every few minutes allows you to reclaim your inner calm.

Yet, staying present doesn't suggest we must disconnect from digital touchpoints. Instead, it's about infusing those interactions with intention. When you next find yourself crafting a message to a new romantic interest, pause. Before that quick tap on "Send," ask yourself—what is the essence of what I want to convey? You'll find that messages sent mindfully often resonate deeper and hold more significance, fostering connections based on authenticity.

In face-to-face meetings, presence involves peeling away layers of distraction. How often, during a meal or coffee chat, do we instinctively check our phones, lulled by routine behavior? Mindful dating encourages undistracted engagement. It asks us to savor the moment, to listen not just to words but to the cadences and emotions behind them. By being truly present, you open the door to genuine understanding and empathy—a solid foundation for any budding romance.

Staying present also involves tuning into the psychological and emotional indicators we may overlook when rushing. Your body and emotions are attuned to subtle cues that signal comfort, interest, or apprehension. Mindfulness helps you detect these signals, enabling you to navigate interactions more adeptly. A raised eyebrow, a hesitated response, or a fleeting smile—each is a treasure map to your partner's authentic narrative.

A practical way to enhance your dating mindfulness is to establish personal rituals before engaging in digital or in-person interactions. These can be simple, like lighting a scented candle, taking a few deep breaths, or jotting down your thoughts in a journal. Rituals act as gentle reminders, turning your focus back to the present and letting each moment unfold with clarity.

Equally important is the intention behind your interactions. Are you genuinely looking to understand and connect with this person, or are you rushing through the motions? Intention acts as the navigator of the mindful dating journey. It centers your actions and helps you align experiences with your authentic desires.

Mindfulness also paves the way for vulnerability, a pivotal component of deep relationships. When we are present, we are open to recognizing and revealing our true selves, free of the filters that can often distort digital communications. This vulnerability is both a gift and a responsibility, as it invites others to be open too, fostering a space where deep, meaningful connections can thrive.

Lastly, consider the rejuvenating simplicity embedded in gratitude practices. In the rush to find someone special, we might overlook the moments of joy that punctuate our dating journey. By taking a moment at the end of each interaction to reflect on something you're grateful for—be it the conversation, laughter, or shared understanding—you reinforce positivity and presence in your dating life. This not only enriches your own experience but also impacts those you encounter.

By staying present in a fast-paced world, we don't just survive the whirlwind of modern dating; we thrive in it. Authentic connections, birthed from mindful practices, have the potential to transcend the transient and touch the eternal. Thus, as we navigate the digital age, let us remember to tether our hearts to the stillness amidst the storm—to truly be in the moment, in love, and in life.

Building Emotional Intelligence

In a world driven by algorithms and constant notifications, finding a partner who genuinely resonates with you can feel elusive. Yet, more than ever, building emotional intelligence is crucial for nurturing meaningful connections. This skill isn't just about identifying our own emotions but also understanding the emotional cues of others, which is key in establishing a deeper, more authentic bond.

Emotional intelligence encompasses a variety of competencies, including self-awareness, self-regulation, empathy, and social skills. Developing these facets allows you to better navigate the ups and downs of dating, helping you manage stress and conflict while fostering stronger, more positive interactions with potential partners. At its core, emotional intelligence is about being present and attentive, something that's often overshadowed by the rush of modern technology.

To begin with, self-awareness is the foundation of emotional intelligence. It involves a thorough understanding of your own emotions, strengths, and weaknesses. By regularly reflecting on your experiences and how they affect your mood and behavior, you grow more attuned to yourself. This self-awareness serves as a compass, guiding you to recognize what you truly seek in a relationship and helping you identify if the connection you're pursuing aligns with your values and desires.

Self-regulation follows closely on the heels of self-awareness. It's all about managing your emotions in a healthy way, ensuring they don't overpower your decisions or lead to regrettable actions. In the dating context, self-regulation helps mitigate impulsive responses, particularly in situations where messages can be misinterpreted or when confronted with the inevitable highs and lows of pursuing a relationship. By practicing mindfulness and patience, you cultivate flexibility and resilience, essential qualities for any successful relationship.

Empathy, another pivotal component of emotional intelligence, involves tuning into the emotions and experiences of others. When you're dating, empathy becomes your superpower, offering you the ability to genuinely connect with your partner by understanding their perspective and feelings. This goes beyond merely listening to what they're saying; it requires you to be present and attentive, picking up on unspoken cues such as body language and tone of voice. Empathy not only strengthens the bond between partners but also minimizes misunderstandings, paving the way for healthier communication and a more profound emotional connection.

Moreover, the social skill aspect of emotional intelligence plays an instrumental role in dating. Being able to effectively communicate your thoughts and feelings, while understanding and valuing your partner's, is a delicate dance that requires practice and patience. Social aptitude allows you to navigate the complexities of relationship dynamics, guiding you to handle conflicts gracefully and engage in meaningful, yet lighthearted, conversations that foster intimacy and trust. In essence, strong social skills are the glue that holds a relationship together.

For those navigating the dating scene today, emotional intelligence offers a unique edge, differentiating shallow, short-lived encounters from substantial, lasting relationships. By cultivating emotional awareness, you are not only enhancing your personal well-being but also enriching your connections, enabling you to identify and align with partners who resonate on a deeper emotional level.

The development of emotional intelligence isn't just for the early, exploratory phase of dating; it's an ongoing journey that continues to enrich relationships long after the initial frisson of attraction has subsided. As you grow alongside your partner, emotional literacy allows you to adapt to changes, manage shared challenges, and celebrate shared triumphs. This adaptability and depth create a strong emotional bond that withstands the test of time.

To nurture emotional intelligence in the dating sphere, practice mindfulness regularly. Mindfulness helps you remain grounded in the present moment, preventing overanalysis and anxiety about the future. It bolsters self-awareness, pacifies heightened emotions, and fosters empathy. Engage in reflective practices such as journaling or meditation to deepen your understanding of personal emotions and reactions.

Additionally, seek feedback actively. Partners are excellent sources of insight, offering alternative perspectives on how your emotions and behaviors may be perceived. Embrace this input as an opportunity for growth, not criticism. It will refine your emotional response and enhance mutual understanding within the relationship.

Lastly, prioritize open communication. Honest dialogue about feelings, fears, and hopes builds a solid emotional foundation. Encourage discussions that explore emotions without the fear of judgment, creating a safe space where both partners feel heard and valued. This openness cultivates trust, an essential pillar in any successful relationship.

In closing, as technology continues to evolve and transform the landscape of dating, the human need for genuine emotional connection remains timeless. By embracing and enhancing your emotional intelligence, you equip yourself with the tools necessary to navigate the road toward meaningful relationships, guiding you to a love that's as enduring as it is fulfilling.

Chapter 18:
When to Swipe Right:
Recognizing Red Flags

In a world where potential connections are just a swipe away, identifying red flags in digital dating can be the key to steering toward meaningful relationships. It's crucial to balance hope with discernment, as profiles brimming with charm can sometimes mask underlying issues. Look beyond the curated photos and clever bios — notice the subtle signals that hint at incompatibility or misrepresentation. Are responses consistently vague or evasive? Is there a reluctance to meet in person, or odd patterns of communication? Trusting your instincts becomes paramount, allowing your intuition to guide you through the digital haze. While hope flutters with every match, recognize when patterns persist that undermine sincerity and genuine connection. Taking a moment to reflect on interactions can shield your heart and open doors to authentic, enriching experiences.

Identifying Warning Signs

As you traverse the captivating landscape of digital dating, it's crucial to develop a discerning eye for warning signs—a skill that can protect your heart while steering you towards genuine connections. In an era where swipes and messages often determine the potential for love, learning to recognize red flags ensures that not only do you guard your emotional well-being, but you also pave the way for more meaningful relationships.

One of the most significant warning signs is inconsistency in communication. If the person you're chatting with one day displays warmth and enthusiasm and then suddenly becomes cold or elusive, it might suggest a lack of genuine interest. Such inconsistencies can often indicate that they are either juggling multiple interests or simply unsure of their intentions. Pay attention to patterns, not just isolated incidents. Do they constantly cancel plans last minute or only message you at odd hours? Inconsistent behavior can signify that someone may not be looking for the same level of commitment or engagement as you are.

Another red flag lies in the way potential partners talk about their past relationships. If conversations frequently return to their ex with a tone of bitterness or blame, it could indicate unresolved issues that might spill over into any new relationship. Listen closely to how they speak about their past; a partner who hasn't moved on emotionally may not be ready to invest fully in something new. On the other hand, if they refuse to discuss their previous experiences altogether, it might suggest a lack of self-reflection or a reluctance to be open and vulnerable.

Beware of those who fast-forward through necessary stages of getting to know each other, leaping into declarations of love or plans for the future almost immediately after your initial interactions. This phenomenon, often called love bombing, is a tactic where someone overwhelms you with attention and affection only to withdraw it unexpectedly. It creates an intense emotional connection that is hard to assess objectively, and such haste should raise questions about their motives and sincerity.

Sometimes, a red flag can be spotted in their unwillingness to introduce you to people they are close to. Meeting friends or family is a natural progression for a relationship that's becoming important, and hesitation or refusal to include you in their lives suggests they might not be as serious as they claim. It can also be indicative of maintaining secrecy or juggling several relationships simultaneously.

Trust your instincts if you notice a reluctance to engage in open and honest dialogue about important topics like relationship goals, lifestyle choices, or future aspirations. Clear and consistent communication is the building block of any healthy relationship. If someone consistently sidesteps meaningful conversations or displays an aversion to discussing the future, it could be a caution about their commitment level.

Be cautious if you detect any controlling behavior. Whether it's excessive inquiry about your whereabouts or a critical attitude towards your friendships, these tendencies start as subtle signs and can evolve into more overtly controlling actions. Paying attention to these early signs can save heartache down the road, as no healthy relationship should involve control or manipulation.

A key indicator of potential problems is when someone evades accountability for their actions. If they're constantly blaming others for their mistakes or failures, it's likely they don't take responsibility in relationships either. Look for someone who can admit when they're wrong and who wants to grow and learn from mistakes. This kind of maturity bodes well for navigating future challenges together.

Don't ignore your instinct if excessive self-centered behavior is evident early on. If every conversation revolves around their achievements, desires, and struggles, with little room for your voice, it may point to a lack of empathy or understanding which makes a partnership difficult. Genuine interest in hearing your thoughts and sharing experiences is a fundamental foundation for intimacy.

In the digital age, a significant red flag can unfold through their digital footprint or lack thereof. A person having minimal or no presence on social media isn't a caution per se, but it might warrant a closer look at their intentions if it's coupled with secretive behavior or inconsistencies in what they tell you. Conversely, an overly curated or exaggerated online persona can also be suspicious as it often aims to mislead.

Trust issues can also arise if you notice excessive flirting with others online. This behavior suggests a lack of exclusivity or seriousness about your budding relationship. While some flirting may be harmless, persistent attention-seeking outside your relationship can be indicative of unmet needs or dissatisfaction.

Lastly, pay heed to the subtleties of your own feelings and reactions. If you find yourself often anxious or second-guessing your worth in the relationship, these emotional responses are sometimes the most telling red flags. Your comfort and confidence are paramount, and someone who truly cares for you should provide reassurance, not reasons for doubt.

Recognizing these warning signs early can prevent the pain of disentangling deeply held emotions later. While everyone has flaws and the potential for red flags is present in all dynamics, the key is to discern which signs are benign quirks and which are serious indicators of incompatibility. With experience and self-awareness, you'll be more adept at distinguishing between them and steering clear of partnerships that might lead to more harm than happiness. By trusting yourself and remaining alert, you're better equipped to navigate toward authentic connections that resonate with your true self in this digital dating era.

Trusting Your Instincts

In the swirling ocean of digital profiles, photos, and carefully crafted bios, it's easy to get caught up in the pursuit of connection without thinking twice. The dopamine rush from each match can cloud your judgment, making it seem like you're always just a swipe away from your next potential partner. But beneath the surface of every profile, there are nuances whispering to your subconscious, urging you to pause and reflect. This is your instinct speaking—your internal compass guiding you amidst the clamor of the dating world.

Understanding and trusting your instincts is more than just a romanticized notion; it's an essential facet of safeguarding your emotions and mental well-being. When navigating the online dating landscape, feelings of trepidation or discomfort often serve as vital signals. Have you ever scrolled through a profile and felt something was off? Maybe the words didn't match the pictures, or their interests seemed performative rather than genuine. Our instincts often pick up on discrepancies before our conscious mind does, and learning to heed these nudges can prevent us from becoming entangled in toxic entanglements.

There are times when your logical brain may urge you to ignore these gut feelings. Perhaps it's because the prospect appears attractive or has appealing qualifications that you consciously desire. However, intuition works through layers of unspoken communication that we've honed over years. Even without verbal cues or facial expressions, the energy of people transcends digital boundaries. It's a symphony where silence speaks volumes. Trusting your instincts means honoring these moments and respecting the signals your intuition is sending you.

To truly harness the power of your instincts, it's crucial to foster a self-awareness that connects you with your inner world. Spend time reflecting on previous experiences, understanding what felt right and what didn't. Maybe there were moments when you overrode your intuition, only to regret it later. These reflections are not just lessons; they are touchstones in your journey, helping you distinguish between genuine connections and fleeting encounters. Cultivating this self-awareness allows you to tune into your feelings more astutely, aligning your actions with your emotional truths.

Consider for a moment how intuition is often perceived in relationships. Society sometimes dismisses gut feelings as irrational or overly emotional. Yet, many would argue that an essential part of romance and connection is acknowledging the unseen and the unspoken. Think about the magic of a silent glance that communicates understanding or the sensation of being fully seen and heard by another. These intangible elements of a relationship are the very things that cannot be forced or fabricated through words alone.

An instinctive reaction might come in the form of uncertainty about someone's tone during messaging, or discomfort when they ask for something you're not ready to share. It could be as subtle as a hesitation before agreeing to meet, or a feeling of relief canceling a date. These are not to be ignored nor judged as paranoia. The value lies in acknowledging these instinctual nudges and exploring their significance. Sometimes, further insight is needed before making a decision. Other times, it's enough just to say no.

When emotions run high and logic grapples for control, how do we differentiate between fear and intuition? This is a common conundrum in dating and often requires self-reflection. Fear stems from past wounds and the anticipation of pain, a protective measure that might limit new experiences. Intuition, in contrast, arises from subtle cues in the present, drawing upon deep-seated knowledge. To discern the two, gently question your response. Ask if your instinctive reaction is rooted in current realities or echoes of what has been before.

Seeing beyond curated profiles means recognizing that everyone embodies a mix of good and bad qualities. Swift judgments based purely on instinct can sometimes block us from meaningful experiences. Therefore, balance is key. Give potential partners the opportunity to reveal their true selves, while also standing firm where your instincts set clear boundaries. The guiding principle should be not to ignore discomfort but to approach it with openness and curiosity. This way, if you choose to lower your guard, it's a choice made with full awareness rather than resignation.

Trust requires practice. Like all facets of love, it grows with continual engagement and honesty. When your instincts steer you right, take note and reinforce that trust. It's a feedback loop, a dance between courage and vulnerability. Gradually, you'll find that this fusion of self-awareness and instinct empowers you to navigate the dating scene with confidence. You're building a robust framework to safeguard your emotional health, ensuring that when you swipe right, it's not just out of hope, but of certainty and readiness.

In essence, learning to trust your instincts is about nurturing your relationship with yourself. It's a tender reminder that you are your first partner, the one who holds you accountable to your truths and desires. As you explore the possibilities of digital dating, remember that each swipe reflects an opportunity to be true to who you are. Trust in yourself becomes the compass that guides you toward what you need, what you want, and ultimately, to the honest love that aligns with both.

Chapter 19:
Building Healthy Digital Relationships

Navigating the digital world of romance calls for thoughtful communication, where words typed on screens can forge connections as deep as those carved face-to-face. It's about crafting a balanced dialogue, understanding not just what to say, but how to listen between the bytes. By setting clear boundaries and respecting them, both parties lay the groundwork for authentic, lasting ties. Digital relationships require a blend of patience and curiosity, where the excitement of learning about each other is matched with the willingness to adapt and grow together. Emphasizing these elements nurtures a partnership that rises above digital distractions, creating a space where love isn't just found, but cherished and cultivated in its healthiest form.

Effective Communication Strategies

Navigating romantic relationships in the digital age can be like exploring a new world—sometimes thrilling and fulfilling, other times daunting and bewildering. At the core of a successful digital relationship is effective communication. While communication remains a foundational component in any relationship, its nuances have evolved with technology. No longer restricted to face-to-face interactions or the rare letter-writing exchanges of the past, today's digital communication happens in bursts of texts, emojis, video calls, and social media exchanges. This new landscape requires a fresh set of strategies to ensure that your message is both clear and constructive, laying the groundwork for healthy and fulfilling connections.

One of the essential elements of effective communication is clarity. In a digital world, where words can easily be misunderstood or taken out of context, being clear about your intentions and feelings is particularly crucial. Texts can lack tone and body language, making it harder to convey sarcasm or humor. To mitigate this, consider using well-placed emojis or explicitly stating your emotions, especially when discussing sensitive topics. It's better to err on the side of overcommunication than to risk misunderstanding. Remember, clarity doesn't just help convey messages accurately; it also builds trust by minimizing assumptions and misinterpretations.

Equally important is active listening, which might seem paradoxical when the exchange is digital rather than face-to-face. However, responding thoughtfully instead of instantly can lead to a more meaningful dialogue. Give yourself time to process what your partner has expressed online, then respond in a manner that acknowledges their feelings and viewpoints. This not only shows respect but also ensures you fully understand what is being communicated. Whether through a text or more immediate exchanges like video chat, creating space for active listening enhances connection and understanding, marking a pivotal step in cultivating a healthy digital relationship.

Emotional intelligence plays a significant role in effective communication. Technology may have changed how we interact, but empathy and emotional awareness are timeless and vital. Tuning into not just the words being said—or typed—but also the underlying emotions can set you apart in the digital dating universe. Reading between the lines and understanding not just what your partner is telling you but how they are feeling cultivates deeper empathy. Through this lens, you can navigate conversations with care, fostering emotional bonds that withstand the transient nature of digital interactions.

Digital conversations demand adaptability. Platforms and methods of communication vary, each with its own set of unspoken rules and norms. Transitioning from texting to video calls, for example, requires altering your communication style and adjusting to visual cues. Embrace flexibility to maintain connection and engagement, tailoring your approach to fit the platform and context. Doing so exhibits respect and understanding for your partner's preferred method of interaction, thereby enhancing the relationship.

Setting the right tone is another pivotal strategy. In digital correspondence, where nuances can get lost amid the brevity, tone becomes more significant. It's easy to come across as curt or indifferent, especially in texts. Being mindful of your partner's communication style and mirroring it where appropriate can help maintain harmony. Including warmth and enthusiasm in your messages can breathe life into a seemingly mundane conversation. Tone, when used effectively, can transform digital communication into something as rich as any face-to-face conversation.

Moreover, embracing honesty is foundational for effective communication. In a world where digital personas can sometimes overshadow authenticity, being truthful and genuine in your interactions builds a solid base for trust and intimacy. Honesty isn't just about sharing truths; it's also about expressing wants, needs, and limits openly. This candor fosters an environment where both partners feel safe to be themselves, paving the way for a more profound connection. In digital spaces where many hide behind screens, your authenticity will be refreshing and magnetic.

Balancing between sharing and over-sharing is a delicate dance in digital communication. It's crucial to be open and vulnerable, but also wise about what and how much you share at different stages of the relationship. Oversharing too soon can overwhelm both you and your partner, setting unrealistic expectations or misplacing trust. Establishing boundaries about personal details and sensitive topics helps create a comfortable pace for relationship growth. This measured approach keeps the relationship in tune with both partners' comfort levels, ensuring space for organic progression.

Conflict in any relationship is inevitable, but it requires more care in the digital world. Resolving disagreements through texts can lead to misinterpretations. Whenever possible, opt for voice or video calls, where tone and expressions add context. In the heat of an argument, resist the impulse to react immediately. Take time to cool down, gather your thoughts, and return to the conversation with a focus on solutions rather than blame. Always aim for resolution over resentment, remembering that the goal is to strengthen, not weaken, your digital bond.

Timing, while subtle, is vital in digital communication. A well-timed message can convey thoughtfulness and attentiveness, making your partner feel valued. Conversely, delayed responses might imply disinterest or distraction. Striking the right balance in response time is an art; too quick, and it might seem over-eager, too slow, and it risks disconnection. By paying attention to the timing of your communications, you demonstrate respect for your partner's emotions and schedules, reinforcing the relationship's quality.

Lastly, fostering communication that supports continuous growth will benefit your relationship. Encourage open dialogues about not just day-to-day experiences but also long-term dreams, fears, and shared goals. These conversations deepen your bond and build a partnership that's resilient to digital distractions. As technology continues to evolve, relationships grounded in effective communication will remain the cornerstone of meaningful connections, adapting and growing alongside these technological advancements.

In conclusion, the digital age offers vast opportunities for connection, but it also demands a higher level of communication competence. By focusing on clarity, active listening, emotional intelligence, adaptability, and honesty, digital relationships can thrive and transform into deeply fulfilling partnerships. Embrace the space where technology and communication meet, and let it be a foundation for building love that's grounded in genuine understanding and mutual respect.

Setting and Respecting Boundaries

In the digital landscape where swipes and dings dictate the tempo of romance, setting and respecting boundaries has become essential. It's like the unsung symphony conductor, guiding interactions that dance between screens. Here, the need for clear borders is paramount—not only to safeguard one's emotional well-being but to cultivate connections that are genuinely fulfilling.

Imagine, for a moment, the vast field of online dating as a series of invisible paths. Each person you encounter carries their own unique trail, a map of emotional triggers and untold stories. In this complex web of connections, establishing personal limits helps to navigate the chaos, ensuring that interactions unfold in ways that are respectful and meaningful.

Think of boundaries as the invisible yet impenetrable curtains around the core of your being. They define the space where others' influence stops and your sense of self begins. By setting these lines, you're not building a fortress of solitude. Rather, you're creating an empowered space where healthy dialogue can exist, free from the threat of emotional tumult.

In the art of modern romance, articulating your boundaries involves honesty and a touch of vulnerability. You can't force someone to understand your limits, but you can communicate them clearly. Simple, declarative expressions like, "I'm comfortable with this," or "This doesn't work for me," can act as the guiding beacons in your digital journey. It's about carving a path that respects your feelings while staying open to genuine connections.

Now, consider the act of respecting others' boundaries. It requires a delicate balance of empathy and awareness. Picture this: an orchestra where one out-of-tune instrument can disrupt the entire melody. Disregarding someone's boundaries has a similar effect, potentially sending ripples of discontent and misunderstanding across the relationship. Instead, listening actively, paying attention to both the spoken and unspoken languages, fosters a climate where mutual respect thrives.

In the fast-paced realm of digital dating, it's easy to ignore the unspoken boundaries. A seemingly innocuous comment or persistent message might overstep another's comfort zone. Thus, mindfulness is crucial—an intentional focus on not only what you say but how it might be received. Practicing patience and gently probing into the preferences of your counterpart can help maintain a respectful equilibrium.

Reflect for a moment on your own experiences. Have there been interactions where boundaries either made or broke the connection? These instances are not mere blips but valuable lessons. Each boundary tests the resilience and adaptability of your relationship skills. By acknowledging missteps without judgment, you grow and evolve in your understanding of relational dynamics.

Remember, boundaries are not static. They adapt and shift, reflective of your ongoing personal growth and changing life circumstances. As digital relationships develop, you might find yourself renegotiating these boundaries in response to new-found intimacy or emotional insight. This evolving nature signifies progress, illustrating the dynamic interplay between two people striving for harmony.

Consider the cultural context in which these online interactions occur. Societal norms, individual backgrounds, and varying communication styles all influence the conception of what boundaries mean. This complexity highlights the importance of being patient with others and yourself as you navigate differing interpretations of personal space.

Technology provides tools and platforms that should, ostensibly, bring people closer. Yet, these very mechanisms can also blur the lines that boundaries strive to maintain. Privacy settings, social media visibility, and mutual acquaintances all necessitate a tailored approach to boundary-setting. Being thoughtful about what you share and with whom is an integral part of constructing a safe emotional environment.

In a world where ghosting and breadcrumbing have become part of the vernacular, boundaries guard against the emotional confusion these behaviors bring. They offer a framework that promotes transparent communication and bolsters trust. They empower you to voice discomfort over vague or hurtful actions, steering the focus toward constructive dialogue.

Building and maintaining healthy digital relationships relies heavily on nurturing this balance between clear articulation and empathetic growth. When you're in tune with both your own needs and those of your counterpart, you're not merely interacting; you're fostering a fertile ground where mutual understanding blossoms. This is the essence of respectful, fulfilling connections in the digital age.

Ultimately, while screens mediate much of today's romantic connections, they cannot dampen the age-old wisdom of self-respect and mutual regard. Authentic love, whether it starts with a swipe or a chance encounter, grows in the garden of conscious boundaries. As you navigate this exciting terrain, find strength in your ability to shape interactions that honor both yourself and those who wish to walk beside you.

Chapter 20:
Love in the Time of Social Change

In a world where societal values are constantly shifting, love has become both a reflection of these changes and a conduit for further evolution. As cultural tides rise and fall, relationships adapt, embodying the fluidity of modern norms and newfound freedoms. People are increasingly embracing diverse expressions of identity, reshaping what it means to connect romantically. Amidst these transformations, the quest for love becomes a journey not just of finding a partner, but of exploring one's place in a rapidly changing society. By understanding and embracing these shifts, individuals can forge deeper connections that transcend traditional boundaries. This dance of love in the time of social change challenges us to remain open-hearted and empathetic, reminding us that at its core, love is a powerful agent of personal and communal transformation.

Adapting to Evolving Norms

The landscape of love and relationships is perpetually shifting, shaped by forces both subtle and profound. As society evolves, so too do the norms governing romantic interactions. Adapting to these changes is not only necessary but can also be incredibly empowering. In an era where technology blurs geographical constraints and cultural exchanges are more fluid than ever, understanding how to navigate evolving norms is crucial for anyone seeking meaningful connections in the modern dating world.

Social change has always influenced relationships. Consider how the feminist movement transformed the expectations and dynamics between partners. Similarly, the recent push for greater gender equality has redefined what partners look for in each other and how they communicate. In today's digital age, the conversation extends beyond gender to include a broader spectrum of identities. Inclusivity and acceptance become important themes as societal norms continue to expand and diversify.

One of the most remarkable consequences of evolving norms is the democratization of love. The barriers that once separated people by race, class, and nationality are slowly dissolving. Dating apps and social platforms have opened the doors to a global pool of potential partners. This mixing pot not only offers a greater variety of choices but also challenges ingrained prejudices and biases, creating a rich tapestry of relationships that would have been unfathomable a few decades ago.

Yet, with all these opportunities come challenges. The swift pace of change can leave some feeling disoriented. What was considered a faux pas yesterday might be celebrated today, and vice versa. The dance of understanding what's considerate, what's permissible, and what's expected is intricate. It requires flexibility and a willingness to continually learn and adapt without losing one's core values and integrity.

Communication plays a pivotal role in adapting to new norms. The way we express interest, resolve conflicts, and articulate needs has had to evolve. From terse text messages to elaborate virtual dates, each mode of communication has its own set of expectations and etiquette. It's crucial to recognize the importance of listening and being open to different styles of interaction, remembering that every relationship is unique and requires its bespoke mode of connection.

In embracing change, one must also understand the importance of self-reflection. It's about recognizing personal biases and being open to introspection. The process can be as enlightening as it is challenging. By reflecting on one's own experiences and comparing them to wider societal shifts, individuals can better understand where they stand and what they truly seek in a partner. This journey of self-discovery can be transformative, fostering growth and deeper connections.

Despite the fluidity of norms, the pursuit of genuine love and connection remains constant. While the methods and environments may change, the fundamental desire to be understood, appreciated, and loved persists. It's this unchanging nature of human emotions that serves as a familiar anchor in the ever-evolving sea of cultural expectations.

Moreover, as we navigate this evolving landscape, empathy becomes an invaluable skill. Understanding and appreciating differences, seeking to learn rather than judge, can help bridge gaps that norms might initially make seem insurmountable. Empathy fosters connections that are deep and authentic, transcending superficial differences.

Finally, it's essential to highlight that evolution in dating norms is not solely about individual change. It's about community, about being part of a collective transformation towards inclusivity and understanding. It's about celebrating love in all its forms and colors, and acknowledging that the diversity of human experiences only enriches the tapestry of relationships. So, as you adapt to these evolving norms, celebrate them. Find strength in your flexibility, wisdom in past experiences, and excitement for the future that continues to unfold.

The Impact of Cultural Shifts

In the whirlwind of modern romance, cultural shifts have become the invisible hands reshaping the landscape of how we connect and thrive in relationships. As society morphs with each passing decade, these transitions leave indelible imprints on our understanding of love and companionship. One could argue that the way we love today is a direct reflection of the larger social movements that have swept across the globe over the years. From changing gender roles to the rise of multicultural and LGBTQ+ acceptance, the cultural dialogues of today actively influence how people navigate the complex world of dating.

With the dissolution of rigid gender roles, relationships have experienced newfound fluidity and freedom. Today, it's not uncommon for partners to share responsibilities equally, a notion that would have been unthinkable only a few generations ago. As the feminist movement continues to dismantle outdated hierarchies, it has also prompted a broader reflection on what equality really means in relationships. Modern love is increasingly built on the foundations of mutual respect and understanding, aspects that are critical for fostering genuine connections.

"Tradition" may once have dictated much about whom we loved and how we expressed it, but contemporary culture has expanded these horizons considerably. The acceptance and celebration of diverse expressions of love, from interracial relationships to those embracing different faiths and backgrounds, are a testament to this shift. The saying "Love knows no boundaries" takes on a much more tangible meaning in a time when societal progress invites us to embrace differences, rather than shy away from them. This cultural climate allows for more meaningful interactions, as individuals feel empowered to pursue relationships that align with their authentic selves.

The impact of these cultural changes is starkly visible in the digital dating arena. As we navigate apps designed to bring us closer, there is an underlying assumption of inclusivity. Platforms now celebrate various orientations, identities, and desires, encouraging users to embrace their unique narratives. This technological shift mirrors and amplifies broader cultural changes, echoing an age where individual stories carry tremendous value. Users from various backgrounds and orientations can now find spaces that acknowledge and validate their experiences, an essential factor in forming connections that truely resonate.

Moreover, with the rise of social activism, many individuals show a growing interest in dating someone who shares or respects their socio-political values. As people become more vocal about their beliefs, their outlook on relationships also evolves. In a world where real-time news and movements emerge overnight, there's a palpable enthusiasm for coupling love with shared missions and values. This cultural phenomenon empowers individuals to engage in relationships where values align closely, adding another layer of depth to what it means to connect in today's day and age.

The cultural renaissance we've encountered isn't without challenges, however. Such seismic shifts often come with tensions and resistance from those who prefer the comforts of old norms. Intergenerational gaps can arise, leading to misunderstandings or hesitations around new dating paradigms. Yet, these challenges serve not just as obstacles but as reminders of the progress still to be made. As we navigate these evolving norms, we're constantly reminded of the need for empathy and open dialogues, essential tools in bridging any divides that may exist.

Every shift carries with it the potential for growth and understanding. As societal norms continue to evolve, one thing remains clear: human connections are dynamic, capable of adapting to the cultural ebbs and flows that define our times. The beauty of these changes lies in their ability to dissolve barriers, enabling love to transcend beyond the conventional and historical limitations that previously defined it.

For many, these changes mean a world of possibilities awaits, a landscape where personal experiences and individual stories build the tapestry of love. By understanding and embracing these cultural shifts, we not only enrich our personal lives but also contribute to a broader movement toward inclusivity and understanding, essential components of any successful relationship in today's world.

Love is not static, nor is it isolated from the cultural context in which it exists. It evolves, it learns, and it grows, much like the individuals who experience it. As we lean into these cultural transformations, we find ourselves at the cusp of not just personal discovery but a collective understanding that love, in its many forms, is one of the greatest adventures of life. In this exploration, we are invited to redefine what romance looks like in our rapidly changing world, forging pathways of connection that are as varied as they are profound.

Chapter 21:
Empowering Women in the
Digital Dating Arena

As the digital dating landscape continues to evolve, women are finding their voices and agency in this modern age of romance. Navigating the intricate web of gender dynamics, many are transforming the way they approach connections, rising above stereotypes and societal expectations. Empowerment comes not just from understanding these dynamics but embracing them with confidence and self-awareness. In this environment, women are encouraged to stand firm in their desires and boundaries, recognizing that authenticity and self-advocacy can forge genuine and fulfilling connections. What's inspiring is the growing community of supportive voices—online and offline—that champion women's experiences, echoing the sentiment that digital dating should be a realm where every woman's narrative is valued and elevated. The possibilities are endless when women harness the power of digital tools, combining intuition with intention to traverse the path of modern love on their own terms.

Navigating Gender Dynamics

In the rapidly evolving realm of digital dating, gender dynamics manifest in new and often unexpected ways. As platforms encourage interactions at a speed that can be both exhilarating and daunting, understanding these dynamics becomes crucial. Women especially find themselves at a unique crossroads where empowerment meets tradition. While digital platforms promise a more level playing field, echoes of established societal norms still reverberate, sometimes subtly influencing perceptions and interactions.

For many, the virtual dating world offers a sense of liberation. Women can take control of their narratives, deciding when and whom to engage with. The algorithms and features of dating apps have, in some ways, democratized dating, allowing women to make the first move with confidence and without fear of societal judgment. This represents a seismic shift from the traditional dating script and opens new possibilities for redefining romantic engagements.

Yet, with greater freedom comes new challenges. The anonymity of the internet, while freeing, can also embolden less savory behaviors. Gender stereotypes sometimes persist, with expectations that women should respond in certain ways or adhere to outdated notions of femininity. Navigating these stereotypes requires a blend of awareness and resilience. It also necessitates the ability to assert one's boundaries and comfort levels firmly and clearly, ensuring that digital dating remains a space of empowerment rather than constraint.

Understanding gender dynamics also means recognizing and challenging the biases coded into these digital platforms. Algorithms that match potential partners might inadvertently perpetuate existing biases, subtly shaping interactions in ways users might not immediately recognize. As women navigate this digital arena, questioning these algorithmic practices is crucial. It's important to push for transparency and fairness, for platforms to evolve in ways that support authentic and equitable connections.

In embracing these challenges, women aren't just participants in the digital dating world—they're architects of a new social landscape. This requires courage, as the task often involves confronting ingrained societal norms and reshaping them. By redefining roles and expectations in the dating sphere, women can create spaces where genuine, fulfilling connections are more than just possible; they become the norm.

The empowerment process is intertwined with fostering self-awareness and embracing authenticity. When women present their true selves in the digital world, they invite connections that transcend superficial interactions. This authenticity serves as a beacon, attracting like-minded individuals who value honesty and genuine engagement. It's about crafting a digital persona that's both true and resonant, allowing authentic connections to flourish.

Moreover, digital dating becomes a platform for self-advocacy, urging women to voice their needs and desires without apology. As women engage in these virtual spaces, they learn to articulate their expectations boldly, enhancing their ability to form relationships built on mutual respect and understanding. It's a journey of discovering one's voice and exercising it with confidence, leading to more satisfying and egalitarian relationships.

In parallel, community-building among women on these platforms can fortify this empowerment. Sharing experiences, supporting each other through challenges, and celebrating triumphs fosters a strong network that can provide encouragement and guidance. This solidarity breaks down competitive myths often associated with dating, creating instead a collective push towards positive change and mutual empowerment.

As women continue to navigate these gender dynamics, technology serves both as a tool and a teaching ground. It drives the need for continuous learning and adaptation. Embracing these dynamics means staying open to change, willing to adjust perspectives, and ready to confront biases whenever they arise. This journey, while challenging, is a rewarding path towards a future where digital dating is inclusive, equitable, and genuinely rewarding for all.

In essence, navigating gender dynamics in the digital dating world is about reclaiming control and steering the dialogue in favor of equality and mutual respect. It challenges traditional paradigms and fosters a space where empowerment transcends the virtual, influencing broader societal interactions. As women become more adept at negotiating this digital terrain, they not only harness the power of technology but also chart new territories for future generations, leaving a legacy of courage and change.

Encouraging Confidence and Self-Advocacy

Building confidence and self-advocacy in digital dating is not merely about grasping the mechanics of swiping right or crafting the perfect profile. It's a deeper journey, a path where empowerment arises from embracing one's true self and communicating that authenticity in the digital realm. This journey starts with self-reflection, understanding personal values, desires, and boundaries. To feel truly empowered, women must first recognize their worth independent of any external validation.

Self-confidence in the dating arena often begins with a deep-seated belief in one's own value. It's essential to appreciate your own qualities and strengths, whether they're rooted in kindness, humor, intelligence, or resilience. This internal acknowledgment is the foundation upon which confidence is built. It allows for honest and open expression, essential in forming meaningful connections. When you approach digital dating with a strong sense of self, each interaction becomes an opportunity to share your uniqueness, rather than a platform for seeking approval.

Successful self-advocacy stems from effective communication. Knowing what you want and need from a relationship allows you to articulate this clearly to potential partners. Communication in digital dating is often challenging; it lacks the non-verbal cues of face-to-face interactions. However, this can also be an advantage. Typed words offer the chance to choose language deliberately, ensuring clarity and honesty. This requires women to assertively express their expectations, preferences, and deal-breakers from the outset.

To bolster confidence and advocacy, it can help to adopt a mindset of abundance. This means recognizing the myriad of possibilities available rather than focusing on scarcity or potential rejections. The fear of rejection can be a significant barrier, yet it's crucial to remember that rejection is not a reflection of one's inherent worth. Instead, it might simply indicate a lack of compatibility. Reframing rejection in this way transforms it into a tool for refining one's search for the right match, encouraging a resilient approach to the ups and downs of digital dating.

A supportive community can play a pivotal role in building confidence. Sharing experiences with friends who are also navigating the digital dating scene can provide reassurance and insight. These conversations can offer new perspectives and collective wisdom, validating both the positive moments and the challenges. Additionally, engaging in activities outside the digital dating sphere—such as hobbies, volunteering, or professional pursuits—also fortifies self-worth and confidence.

Another critical aspect of self-advocacy in the digital dating world is the ability to recognize and manage biases and power dynamics. Digital platforms sometimes mirror societal imbalances, and being aware of these allows women to navigate interactions with intentionality. This awareness helps manage expectations and fosters a proactive approach to dating, where personal autonomy guides decisions rather than external pressures.

It's also important to maintain a balance between vulnerability and self-protection. Sharing parts of yourself authentically invites genuine connections, but it's equally crucial to safeguard emotional wellbeing.

Setting boundaries—both emotional and practical—is a key component of self-advocacy. This might mean pacing the disclosure of personal information or deciding when to move from online to face-to-face interactions. These boundaries reinforce the idea that your comfort and safety are paramount.

Reflecting on past dating experiences can also boost confidence and promote self-advocacy. Taking time to identify patterns, both positive and negative, provides clarity on what you desire in future relationships. This process can be enlightening, transforming previous setbacks into growth opportunities. Understanding what has and hasn't worked in the past offers a roadmap for future interactions, helping to approach new connections with both optimism and realism.

Ultimately, the goal is to be your own best advocate. This means not compromising on your values or diminishing yourself to fit into someone else's idea of who you should be. True confidence shines through when you remain steadfast in your identity, and self-advocacy flows naturally when you're grounded in your own truth. Encouraging women to embrace these traits within the digital dating environment fosters a culture of respect, empowerment, and genuine connection.

In a world where superficial interactions are easy to come by, maintaining authenticity offers a refreshing counterbalance. When women confidently assert their individuality and advocate for their needs, they help redefine the digital dating landscape. This shift creates a space where genuine connections can flourish, built on mutual respect and shared understanding. Encouraging confidence and self-advocacy in digital dating is more than an individual endeavor; it has the potential to impact broader cultural norms, steering digital interactions toward a more positive and inclusive future.

Chapter 22:
The Future of Digital Dating

As we look toward the future of digital dating, we're at an intersection where innovation and intimacy meet, crafting new pathways for connection. Emerging technologies, from AI-driven matchmaking to immersive virtual reality dates, promise to redefine how we experience romance in the digital age. These advances hold the potential to make encounters more personalized, fostering deeper connections despite physical distances. Yet, navigating this landscape will also demand a heightened awareness of authenticity and intention, ensuring that our quest for love doesn't lose its humanity in the sea of algorithms and screens. The promise of the future is a tapestry woven with both excitement and caution, urging us to embrace innovation while staying grounded in the timeless essence of human connection.

Emerging Trends and Technologies

As we stand on the cusp of a new era in digital dating, it's essential to acknowledge the dramatic transformations shaping how we form connections. Emerging trends and technologies continue to redefine romance in the digital age, offering exciting opportunities for meaningful engagement while presenting new challenges to navigate.

One of the most compelling developments is the incorporation of artificial intelligence (AI) in dating apps. AI is not just an impersonal algorithm sorting through potential matches based on past swipes; it's evolving into a more dynamic confidante, almost like a digital wingman. By analyzing vast amounts of data, AI systems can now provide personalized suggestions, enhance matchmaking accuracy, and even assist in crafting conversation starters. Moreover, with natural language processing capabilities, AI can help interpret the nuances of digital communication, aiming to bridge gaps in human interaction.

Virtual reality (VR) and augmented reality (AR) technologies are also making waves in the dating landscape. These immersive experiences offer an opportunity to transcend the traditional boundaries of digital dating. Imagine going on a virtual date where you visit the Louvre or hike through the Andes, all from your living room. Such experiences not only bring a new dimension to getting to know someone but also challenge the conventional definition of a date. With AR enhancements, users can keep engaging face-to-face interactions, including fun and playful elements that infuse dates with spontaneity and creativity.

Privacy remains a volatile issue, but technology is stepping up to provide solutions here too. Blockchain technology, known for its decentralized and secure nature, is seeping into the dating scene to enhance user privacy and data protection. It offers users control over their personal data, heightening confidence in the platforms they choose. This development is significant as it symbolizes a shift towards more user-centric policies, where comfort and safety underpin the search for love.

Beyond technological advancements, there's a rising trend towards apps catering to niche interests and communities. These platforms foster inclusiveness and provide users with a curated environment that matches their specific lifestyle choices or value systems, such as veganism, environmental activism, or even dog lovers' groups. By honing in on these communities, daters aren't just looking for compatibility; they're searching for alignment in broader life philosophies, adding depth to the pursuit of connection.

Dating apps are also leveraging real-time data to enhance user experience. Geolocation features now intersect with events and activities, offering opportunities for spontaneous meetups or shared experiences. This shift towards 'event-driven' dating allows users to connect over common interests, bringing an element of the unexpected back into dating—a refreshing counterpoint to the predictable nature of swiping. It adds an element of serendipity reminiscent of chance encounters in the physical world.

As the digital dating sphere grows, so does the influence of social media. Many platforms now double as social networks, blurring the lines between friendship and romantic interest. Users can explore profiles rich with content, storytelling, and social interaction before deciding to pursue a relationship. This integration fosters a slower, more organic approach to connection-building, echoing traditional methods where relationships unfolded within shared social circles or community events.

Gamification is another trend catching on in the dating world. By incorporating game-like elements into their platforms—such as quests, challenges, or reward systems—developers aim to make the process of finding a partner more engaging and less daunting. Gamification isn't merely for fun; it plays a role in reducing anxiety, encouraging participation, and fostering a communicative environment. It might transform the sometimes awkward experience of progressing from messaging to meeting into an adventurous journey.

Voice technology is also making strides in transforming how users interact on dating platforms. The intimacy of hearing someone's voice can offer a richer, more nuanced layer to connections, available at the tap of a button. This technology encourages more authentic interactions and offers a glimpse into a person's personality that text alone can't convey. By building connections with the cadence and tone of spoken words, voice technology invites a closeness that bypasses the limitations of text-based communication.

While the innovation is relentless, what remains constant is the timeless quest for love and connection. As future trends unfurl, the challenge lies in navigating this complex landscape without losing sight of what's paramount: authenticity, mutual respect, and genuine connection. In a realm where hearts meet through screens, these emerging technologies and trends remind us that, ultimately, it's the human element—that sincere emotional bond—that leads to rewarding and fulfilling relationships.

In conclusion, the future of digital dating is ripe with possibilities. The intertwining of technology with the foundational elements of love and relationships creates a landscape where possibilities are vast and varied. Embracing these changes with an open heart and mind can lead to profound personal growth and meaningful connections. As these technological trends unfold, the journey of finding love continues to evolve, inviting us all to adapt, learn, and thrive in the ever-changing digital heartspace.

Predicting the Next Evolution of Connection

The digital landscape, in its relentless evolution, is turning into more than just a mere facilitator for fleeting connections. With each swipe and click, it weaves a complex tapestry of human relationships, defining how we perceive romance in an era that values data as much as it does emotion. The next wave of digital dating is poised to transcend beyond just matching algorithms and virtual profiles; it's likely to redefine how we connect with others on a profound and meaningful level. As technology continues to integrate into every nook of our personal lives, it's high time we delve into what the future holds for love in this digital age.

As technology advances, dating platforms will likely leverage these innovations to offer deeper connections. Think beyond swipes and taps; we're on the brink of entering an era where artificial intelligence and machine learning don't just facilitate matches but create intuitive and personalized experiences that mimic human understanding. From recognizing nuanced emotional cues to predicting compatibility based on subtle behaviors, AI is set to revolutionize how connections are made. Imagine a scenario where an algorithm not only suggests potential partners but does so by deeply understanding your life's story and evolving desires. It's not just about likes and dislikes anymore, but about truly getting to know each user on a personal level.

Virtual and augmented reality are also anticipated to play significant roles in crafting immersive dating experiences. Imagine embarking on a virtual date where you can explore a beautiful island together or admire the stars from a serene landscape, all without leaving your living room. These technologies promise to bring a sense of presence and intimacy that video calls can only dream of. Not only do they bridge the geographical divides, but they also add a layer of shared experiences and adventure which can strengthen bonds in unprecedented ways.

Yet, with these advancements come challenges. As technology becomes more enmeshed in our lives, finding the balance between digital interactions and genuine human experiences will be crucial. It's a delicate dance of embracing the new while holding firm to what makes love profoundly human—trust, vulnerability, and deep emotional connections. As we tread into these uncharted territories, we must remain mindful of preserving authenticity within our increasingly digital interactions.

Furthermore, the ethical implications of these advancements will demand our attention. Privacy issues, data security, and consent will become even more paramount as AI and VR collect expansive amounts of personal data to tailor and enhance user experience. The success of future digital dating platforms will hinge not just on their technological prowess, but also on their commitment to ethical standards that protect and empower users.

Moreover, as digital spaces become increasingly inclusive, future platforms will focus more on catering to diverse groups, celebrating unique identities, and creating safe urban online environments where every love story is possible. This progress will dismantle old paradigms and open avenues for love that were once considered unconventional. Through these advancements, technology could play a pivotal role in fostering more inclusive societies where different perspectives and relationships are recognized and valued.

In the future, emotional intelligence will intertwine with digital dating platforms, where understanding and interpreting emotions accurately could be as simple as clicking a button. This development will not only help identify compatibility but also aid in building healthier and more empathetic relationships. Imagine a world where a platform can gauge the emotional needs of its users, offering insights and suggestions on how to nurture and grow their connections. It pushes beyond meeting 'the one'; it's about understanding how to thrive together genuinely.

As we forecast these advancements, it's important to recognize that, at its core, the next evolution of connection is about enhancing our human experience. Technology might change the mediums through which we connect, but it won't replace the inherent desire for meaningful connections. People will continue seeking methods to express vulnerability, support, and love, using technology as a tool rather than a barrier.

The journey to the future of digital dating is not about replacing human interaction but enriching it. The key is in navigating this new world with consciousness, curating experiences that respect individuality while cherishing collective growth. How we choose to adapt to these changes will determine not only the success of these platforms but also the quality of our connections.

In conclusion, the path forward invites excitement and anticipation for what's possible. The potential for future connections exceeds what technology alone can offer. It involves blending innovation with empathy, leveraging new tools while nurturing the timeless aspects of love. As we stand on the brink of this evolution, we embrace the notion that technology and humanity are not at odds but partners on this remarkable journey towards deeper, more meaningful relationships in the digital realm.

Chapter 23:
The Role of Therapy in Modern Relationships

In the tapestry of today's relationships, therapy shines as a beacon of hope and understanding, helping individuals and couples navigate the intricate dance of connection in a tech-driven world. As traditional dating rituals evolve, therapy offers a sanctuary for self-discovery and emotional growth, transforming how we perceive and engage with love. By offering guidance tailored to the complexities of modern romance, therapy empowers us to unearth deeper, more authentic connections. It's an invitation to pause and reflect amidst the whirlwind of possibilities that digital dating presents, fostering resilience and empathy. In embracing this supportive space, couples and singles alike can cultivate a balanced view of their desires and challenges, addressing hidden fears and nurturing a conscious, compassionate approach to relationships.

Seeking Guidance and Support

Navigating modern relationships, with all their complexities and technological influences, can feel daunting at times. As the landscape of romance transforms, the role of therapy has become increasingly pivotal. Therapy offers a guiding light for those seeking clarity, understanding, and deeper connection. More than ever, individuals are turning to professional guidance to navigate the challenges of digital dating and maintain fulfilling relationships.

In an era where connections can be made with a single swipe, the emotional weight of choices and experiences can become overwhelming. Here, therapy serves as a vital tool, providing strategies for self-awareness, communication, and emotional regulation. It's not just about resolving conflicts; therapy encourages exploration of one's values and desires, helping individuals align their romantic endeavors with personal goals and authentic selves.

One of the most profound benefits of therapy is the safe space it offers. This space is crucial for exploring one's feelings, dissecting past experiences, and understanding their impact on current relationship patterns. This process of introspection often leads to revelations that empower individuals to break free from destructive cycles and forge healthier paths forward. As a result, therapy can be transformative, fostering growth and propelling love toward a more fulfilling and genuine axis.

Embarking on therapeutic journeys isn't limited to those in a relationship crisis. Many people proactively seek therapy to enhance their emotional intelligence and relational skills, ensuring they're equipped to handle the nuances of modern love. Whether for individual growth or within the context of a couple, therapy encourages the development of empathy, accountability, and the art of balancing personal needs with those of a partner.

For individuals navigating the dating world, therapy can also be instrumental in dismantling the myths and misconceptions perpetuated by digital dating cultures. The pressure to present a perfect image online or conform to societal expectations can be overwhelming. Therapy can help individuals learn to embrace authenticity, both in how they portray themselves online and in the connections they seek. By identifying and honoring their true selves, individuals can foster more meaningful and lasting relationships.

Moreover, therapy encourages users to develop healthier perspectives about rejection and failure, which are inevitable in the dating landscape. By reframing these experiences as growing opportunities rather than personal failings, therapy equips individuals with resilience and optimism. This mindset shift can be a powerful motivator as individuals continue their pursuit of happiness and love.

For couples, therapy can serve as a foundation for ongoing relationship maintenance. Just like a car needs regular check-ups, relationships can benefit from periodic evaluations. Therapy provides couples with tools to enhance communication, address unmet needs, and navigate life's transitions together. It's a space where both parties can express gratitude, concerns, and hopes for the future, strengthening the bonds that keep them united.

Technology, for all its advantages, has introduced new kinds of challenges into relationships, making therapy even more crucial. Digital communication can sometimes lead to misunderstandings, and the constant influx of information may fuel insecurities and doubts. Therapy assists in navigating these realities by encouraging open dialogue and reinforcing trust through intentional and mindful practices.

A significant aspect of seeking guidance through therapy is the opportunity for self-reflection it provides. This aspect of therapy is essential in helping individuals understand why they make certain choices in their romantic lives. By recognizing how past experiences or subconscious beliefs shaped their behaviors, individuals can become more intentional in creating the future they desire. Therapy encourages wrestling with difficult questions about one's relationship history, ultimately leading to more informed and conscious decisions.

In the end, the pursuit of love is a deeply personal journey, defined by discoveries both delightful and daunting. Seeking guidance through therapy acts as a companion on this journey, illuminating paths forward and helping individuals and couples construct a narrative that's uniquely their own. It's about cultivating connections not only with others but within oneself—a preparation for the boundless potential of modern relationships.

For those feeling overwhelmed or isolated in their relationship struggles, reaching for support can be the first step toward healing and growth. By embracing the wisdom and insights therapy offers, individuals can redefine their relationship scripts and thrive amidst the ever-changing tides of contemporary romance. As therapy becomes an integral part of building relationships, it brings hope and possibility, inspiring individuals to face the future with courage and love.

Incorporating Self-Reflection

When we talk about the role of therapy in modern relationships, it becomes immediately clear that self-reflection is a cornerstone of this process. Self-reflection is not just about glancing inward occasionally; it's an ongoing dialogue with ourselves. It's the fraternal twin of self-awareness, and together, they form the foundation upon which healthy relationships are built.

Think of self-reflection as a mirror that reflects not just who we think we are, but who we truly are—flaws and all. In today's fast-paced world, particularly in the realm of digital dating, it's easy to lose sight of our authentic selves amidst the flurry of profiles, messages, and matches. Self-reflection helps in clearing away this digital clutter, offering clarity and insight.

The therapeutic space offers a unique environment where self-reflection can thrive. It's a sanctuary, free from judgment, where individuals can explore their thoughts and feelings deeply. Often, we hold perceptions of ourselves that aren't based in reality. Therapy helps challenge those perceptions, offering new perspectives. As this veil of illusion begins to lift, self-reflection becomes a powerful ally, encouraging authenticity.

It's crucial to remember that self-reflection is not a solitary endeavor. In the context of therapy, it involves interaction—conversations with a professional who can guide the process. This exchange of ideas can illuminate aspects of our personality and behaviors that might remain obscured without the light of another's insight. It's a collaborative effort towards self-betterment.

Moreover, self-reflection is intertwined with the concept of personal growth. By recognizing patterns in our behavior and identifying areas where change is needed, we empower ourselves to improve not only our romantic relationships but also our interactions across all realms of life. When we understand our triggers and emotional responses, we foster more fulfilling and less reactive relationships.

Incorporating self-reflection into romance, especially in the digital age, requires deliberate effort. The nature of online dating often encourages superficial connections. Quick judgments made by swipes left or right make it easy to bypass the introspection that grounds meaningful relationships. By consciously engaging in self-reflection, we counter this superficiality, focusing instead on sincerity.

Ask yourself: What do I truly seek in a partner, and why? What patterns from past relationships am I repeating? This reflective questioning allows you to dig beneath surface-level preferences, reaching the core of your desires. By understanding these, you're better equipped to seek relationships that align with your true needs, rather than fleeting wants.

One practical way to exercise self-reflection is through journaling. Documenting your dating experiences, feelings, and thoughts provides a tangible way to revisit and assess your emotional landscape. Over time, patterns emerge—perhaps the repeated choice of unavailable partners or a tendency to self-sabotage when romance becomes too real. Therapy facilitates this process by asking probing questions, challenging assumptions, and offering new ways of thinking.

However, self-reflection is not without its challenges. Facing one's fears and vulnerabilities can be daunting. It involves courage to confront uncomfortable truths about ourselves. Yet, in embracing this discomfort, we unlock potential for real transformation. It's important to approach self-reflection with kindness and patience, avoiding self-criticism that can stymie growth.

Therapists often encourage seeing self-reflection as a ongoing journey, not a destination. The changes it promotes aren't instant. They unravel gradually, leading to subtle yet profound shifts in how we view ourselves and engage with the world. Relationships, then, can develop on a more stable and genuine foundation.

In this reflective process, it becomes evident that understanding oneself deeply is the best gift you can offer a partner. It establishes a groundwork of trust and openness. When both individuals in a relationship engage in self-reflection, the partnership can evolve into a synergistic union, where each person supports the other's growth.

As digital dating continues to evolve, its landscape becoming ever more complex, the importance of self-reflection grows. It's the anchor that keeps us moored to our authentic selves amidst the swirling change. By prioritizing self-reflection, we ensure that our journeys in love aren't just about connection, but connection that enriches and sustains us.

In conclusion, the modern dating world, enhanced by the pervasive influence of technology, offers limitless possibilities but also unprecedented challenges. Self-reflection, as fostered within therapeutic settings, becomes an essential tool. It not only enhances our dating experiences but also reinforces the strength and resilience of our romantic relationships. By consistently engaging with ourselves in this way, we foster genuine connections that hold the promise of lasting fulfillment.

Chapter 24:
Success Stories from the Digital Frontier

In the bustling world of digital dating, love often blooms in the most unexpected places, transcending screens to forge lasting, meaningful connections. Take Emily and Jake, who met over a shared love for obscure 1980s rock ballads on a music-centric app. What started as a playful exchange of song recommendations soon developed into a deep bond that defied pixels and distance. Across the globe, Malik and Aisha leveraged technology to keep their spark alive while geography kept them apart, finding solace in video calls and virtual tours of cities they dreamed of exploring together. These stories remind us that while our devices are the springboards, it's our shared values, passions, and timing that weave the fabric of success in the digital romance arena. Such happy couples teach us that amidst the swipes, pings, and pixels, there's room for authenticity and a love as real as any penned in an epic romance or whispered across candle-lit tables.

Real-Life Tales of Lasting Love

The digital landscape of love stories often resembles a patchwork quilt, stitched together with moments of serendipity, vulnerability, and the courage to reach out from behind a screen. Take, for instance, Mia and Jake, who initially crossed paths on a popular dating app. Amidst countless profiles, it was Jake's witty take on a classic novel that caught Mia's attention. What began as an exchange of favorite book passages blossomed into a digital courtship that transcended geographical barriers. Their story reminds us that within the chaos of swipes and matches, there lies the possibility for profound connections; it's just a matter of finding the right thread to tug at.

Within the buzzing realm of online dating, the tale of Arjun and Emily speaks volumes about enduring love. They were from different continents and their lives initially intersected through a forum dedicated to travel enthusiasts. Encouraged by mutual friends they had never met in person, their online discussions gradually revealed shared dreams and values. Yearning to bridge the gap, they arranged their first meeting in a city neither had been to before—a testament to their adventurous spirit. This decision proved pivotal, cementing a love story that has since spanned five years and counting. Arjun and Emily's journey highlights how, even in the digital world, trust and shared adventures can form the foundation of lasting love.

Sarah and Thomas's story is possibly one of the most heartwarming encounters. Striking a connection through a virtual art workshop during a time when in-person interactions were challenging, their bond grew over shared creativity and imagination. Each painting and drawing carried snippets of their personality, unraveled with every brushstroke on virtual canvases. Over time, their discussions evolved beyond art, and into deeper realms of aspirations and fears. When they finally met face-to-face, it felt like reuniting with an old friend, one they had known for years rather than weeks. This shows that love knows no bounds and that sometimes, it finds its beginning in shared passions nurtured in the digital world.

Then there's the intriguing narrative of David and Priya, who uncovered their connection through a social media mix-up. Priya had intended to message a close friend but inadvertently sent a culinary query to David. Thankfully, David, an amateur chef, responded graciously. Their subsequent banter over recipes and cooking tips sparked an unexpected friendship. The appealing aroma of humor and empathy cooked up between them was aromatic enough to transform chance into choice. Eventually, this meaningful mistake paved the way to a robust relationship solidified by a shared zest for life and a pinch of humor—proving that sometimes, our missteps lead us to where we're meant to be.

After several failed meetings and disenchanted texts, Carla and Hugo were on the verge of giving up on dating apps. Yet, during an existential evening tête-à-tête with a glass of wine, Carla stumbled upon Hugo's profile while seeking nothing more than inspiration. His profile, devoid of embellishments and resonating honesty, stood out like a beacon amongst a sea of pretense. They both yearned for sincerity, which became apparent through their candid conversations and meandering discussions. Their love story unfolded as a testament to the power of authenticity in a world often veiled by filters and facades. For Carla and Hugo, cutting through the noise allowed their true selves to connect genuinely and meaningfully.

The digital frontier has also witnessed reconnections, such as the rekindling of Steffi and Ben's high school friendship. Their paths had diverged but serendipity had other plans, and it nudged them to swipe right on a familiar name. Their first virtual chat was reminiscent of yesteryears, filled with playful nostalgia and an eagerness to catch up. As they traversed the streams of shared history, they uncovered a deeper affection that had been dormant all those years. Steffi and Ben illustrate that sometimes, the fabric of past connections can be woven into a future of renewed love.

Juggling cultural differences, Miguel and Hana's narrative is a fascinating story of love triumphing over obstacles. They first met in the expansive online universe, where conversations over language exchange apps unfolded. As they helped one another hone language skills, their discussions transitioned from classroom dialogues to profound connections. Their passage from strangers to partners was paved with challenges of language barriers and cultural differences, yet they stood testament to the belief that love is a universal language transcending all boundaries.

These real-life tales are the bedrock of lasting love emanating from the digital frontier, a testament that technology, when utilized intentionally, can cultivate genuine connections. They remind us that while the platforms facilitate introduction, it is the courage to be open, authentic, and vulnerable that truly fosters intimacy. The stories of these couples inspire hope and fortitude, resonating with anyone navigating the terrain of modern dating, seeking not just a partner, but a confidante and a companion in love and life.

While each love story is unique, these digital successes share common threads of open communication, shared interests, and deep commitment. The digital frontier may seem daunting with its vast array of options, but within the tumult, lasting love stories like those of Mia and Jake, Arjun and Emily, and others emerge as beacons of hope, demonstrating what's possible when serendipity and sincerity align. Their narratives affirm that the pursuit of love, although fraught with uncertainties, is always enriched with the promise of discovery, joy, and for some, a lifetime of togetherness.

Lessons Learned from Happy Couples

In the expansive digital landscape of modern romance, real-life tales of lasting love provide both a blueprint and a beacon. Happy couples who've met online offer us not just stories of connection, but a tapestry of lessons woven from their experiences. These stories show that while the route to love might have changed, the destination remains the same—deep, committed relationships.

One of the first lessons we've gathered from these couples revolves around adaptability. Technology has opened new avenues for connection, but it also demands flexibility. Couples who successfully navigate the digital dating scene often talk about the importance of being open to unexpected opportunities. By embracing new platforms and technologies, they found love in places they might not have considered initially. This open-mindedness allowed them to explore diverse connections which, against the odds, blossomed into meaningful relationships.

Communication, as many happy couples stress, is another crucial factor. The art of communicating effectively transcends the medium, be it a text message or a video call. Couples in successful digital relationships prioritize clear dialogue, expressing their needs and expectations from the outset. They say that while emojis and GIFs add flavor to conversations, real connection requires words—carefully chosen and thoughtfully conveyed. It's these conversations that build the foundation of understanding, paving the way for deeper emotional intimacy.

Moreover, developing a shared vision of the relationship's future appears vital. Happy couples note that discussing long-term goals early on prevents misunderstandings later. These discussions, often initiated online, allow partners to gauge compatibility and align their aspirations. By dreaming together, they've built a path forward that caters to both personal ambitions and mutual growth.

There is also a lesson in patience. Navigating the digital realm can be overwhelming, with its seemingly infinite choices and fast-paced interactions. Happy couples remind us that meaningful relationships take time. The initial online exchange might spark interest, but true connection requires nurturing over time. They speak of patience not just with each other, but also with themselves as they navigate what they truly want in a partner and a relationship.

Resilience is another theme that emerges from their stories. Many couples face challenges unique to online dating: long-distance separations, digital miscommunications, and the prevalent culture of casual flings. Those who've triumphed reveal that resilience helped them weather such storms. By putting in the effort to overcome obstacles, they forged stronger bonds and learned more about each other's strength and loyalty.

The digital age has redefined trust, a component pivotal to these success stories. Trust now extends beyond fidelity; it includes confidence in digital privacy, honesty in online portrayals, and integrity in communication. Excelling couples have discovered ways to build and maintain trust online, understanding that transparency and consistent efforts are key. They've shared passwords, met friend circles from afar virtually, and used technology to reinforce commitment, not undermine it.

Additionally, the importance of maintaining individuality resonates in their narratives. While it might be tempting to merge lives entirely in a digital dating context, maintaining personal interests and friendships remains crucial. Couples highlight how preserving personal space aids in preventing dependency and fostering a healthier partnership. They balance time spent together with personal pursuits, ensuring that the relationship adds to, rather than solely defines, their happiness.

Finally, successful digital couples make time for offline interactions, whether that's through scenic picnics, afternoon coffee dates, or shared hobbies. They realize that while their relationship might have begun online, solidifying their connection in the physical world is just as important. These moments, tangible and real, help ground their journey and provide nourishing memories to look back on.

In essence, the stories of happy couples charting their course through digital waters demonstrate that love indeed knows no boundaries—not even the intangible ones of pixels and data. They've carved their paths with adaptability, open communication, patience, resilience, trust, individuality, and a seamless blend of online and offline interactions. These lessons embrace the spirit of the digital frontier while honoring the timeless traditions of love and commitment. As we navigate this evolving landscape, these stories inspire us to remain optimistic and open-hearted, trusting that the essence of love stays evergreen amidst the digital revolution.

Chapter 25:
Designing Your Personal Love Strategy

As we journey through the intricate pathways of modern romance, it's crucial to carve out a strategy uniquely tailored to you—a love strategy that embodies both your personal aspirations and heart's desires. This chapter isn't just about making love happen; it's about cultivating a deeper understanding of what truly fulfills you. Start by setting clear intentions, envisioning the qualities that matter most in a partner, and considering the type of relationship that genuinely nourishes your spirit. This intentional approach helps clarify not just who you're looking for, but why. As you sketch this plan, include practical steps to weave authenticity and commitment into your interactions, all while embracing the spontaneity that love so often brings. Remember, love is not a destination but a journey; every swipe, conversation, and gesture is a step toward the meaningful connection that awaits. Equip yourself with the courage to stay true to your values, the wisdom to discern genuine opportunities, and the resilience to learn from each experience. With heart and mind aligned, your personal love strategy becomes a compass guiding you through the digital dating landscape, leading you to experiences as unique as your own fingerprint.

Setting Intentions and Goals

Finding love in the digital age often seems like a quest straight out of a modern fairy tale, complete with its magical worlds of algorithms and endless choices. Yet, where does one really begin on this journey? It's surprisingly simple: start with setting intentions and goals. Like any worthwhile endeavor, designing a personal love strategy requires clarity of purpose, guided by self-reflection and a deep understanding of what you truly want in a relationship. This section delves into the art of consciously shaping your romantic future by looking within and setting meaningful objectives.

Understanding your intentions begins with introspection. Start by asking yourself these fundamental questions: What are you looking for in a partner? What kind of relationship do you envision? Are you ready for a serious commitment, or are you seeking companionship and fun without strings attached? It may sound simple, but these questions call for honesty and self-awareness, as they form the foundation upon which your love strategy stands. It's about knowing your heart's desires and not just following trends or succumbing to societal pressures.

The next step is aligning your intentions with achievable goals. Think of intentions as the guiding lights that illuminate your path, whereas goals are the concrete steps you'll take to reach your aspirations. An intention might be to find a partner who inspires personal growth, and a corresponding goal could be engaging in activities or joining communities where such individuals are likely to be found. Goals serve as milestones, marking your progress and keeping you motivated on days when the digital dating scene feels overwhelming.

Crafting these intentions and goals is not about setting rigid parameters; it's more about establishing a flexible roadmap. Circumstances and feelings evolve, and so too can your objectives. Staying adaptable is key. For example, you might begin with the intention of fostering long-term love but discover along the way that meaningful friendships or short-term relationships align more closely with your current life stage or emotional needs.

Equally important is distinguishing between wants and needs. In a partner and relationship, what are your non-negotiables? These are intrinsic values that you can't compromise on, like shared core beliefs or mutual respect. Wants are preferences that add to the relationship but aren't essential, such as specific hobbies or lifestyles. By setting goals that prioritize needs over wants, you ensure that your strategy leads you toward fulfilling and satisfying connections, rather than superficial or temporary ones.

Let's explore how intention-setting intersects with authenticity. Bringing your sincere self into any relationship increases the chance of forming genuine ties. It means being honest about who you are and what you stand for, which in turn attracts individuals looking for someone just like you. Moreover, authenticity fosters trust and deeper connections. As such, an intention might focus on being unapologetically true to yourself at all times, where a related goal could be ensuring your online dating profile genuinely reflects your personality rather than an aspirational version of yourself.

Achieving these goals requires consistency and perseverance. Success doesn't always happen overnight, especially in the realm of love. It involves a commitment to put in the necessary effort without becoming discouraged by setbacks or rejections, which are parts of the journey and offer valuable lessons along the way.

Remember that setting goals is not about succumbing to a stringent checklist but rather guiding you to thrive in a supportive and emotionally fulfilling relationship. It allows you to be deliberate in your choices, seeking partners and experiences aligned with your greater life aspirations. You are crafting a living, breathing strategy that evolves as you do, embracing the journey of love with open-mindedness and heart.

As you set out on this path, embrace the uniqueness of your timeline. Love isn't a race, and comparing your journey to others' only distracts from the pursuit of what truly matters to you. Trust in your process, knowing that each step forward, no matter how small, brings you closer to the relationship you've envisioned.

Ultimately, setting intentions and goals in your love life empowers you to take an active role in shaping your romantic destiny rather than leaving it to chance. It's about living with purpose, embracing the possibilities the digital world offers while remaining grounded in your values and desires. With clear intentions and well-aligned goals, you're not just searching for love; you're inviting it into your life. The digital dating landscape becomes a realm of opportunities, where each interaction is a stepping stone toward that meaningful connection you've thoughtfully prepared yourself to receive.

Creating a Fulfillment Plan

Embarking on a journey through the labyrinth of modern dating can feel both exhilarating and daunting. The dazzling array of options that technology offers often leaves us teetering between hope and hesitation. Yet, the essence of a truly rewarding romantic life requires more than just chance encounters on apps or serendipitous meetings at bars. It calls for a deeper, more introspective approach—an intentional blueprint that guides us towards not just finding love, but cultivating a genuinely fulfilling connection.

A fulfillment plan in the context of love is akin to designing a roadmap for a journey. It's about aligning your romantic pursuits with your personal values, desires, and long-term aspirations. Imagine it as constructing a home; the foundation is laid by self-awareness and authenticity, walls are built with communication, and the roof is cemented by mutual respect and shared dreams. Without these components, love can become a series of fleeting encounters that never quite fill the heart's longings.

To start crafting your fulfillment plan, first dedicate time to understanding what fulfillment truly means to you in the realm of love. For some, it's about shared adventures and deep conversation; for others, it might be about a quiet companionship that feels like home. Reflection is key here. Consider moments from past relationships that brought you genuine happiness or contentment. Note these experiences as focal points, guiding stars that direct you towards what you truly seek.

Next, transform these reflections into actionable goals. This process is not about creating a checklist of traits for an ideal partner— those tend to restrict rather than liberate. Instead, focus on the experiences and emotional states you wish to cultivate. Do you crave intellectual exchange or perhaps emotional security? Prioritize these desires, allowing them to inform the choices you make and the people you pursue. It's less about setting rigid milestones and more about crafting a dynamic framework that evolves with your understanding of self and others.

Commitment to growth stands at the heart of a fulfillment plan. In relationships, both parties are in a constant state of evolution, learning and growing from individual and shared experiences. Recognize that achieving fulfillment may require you to step beyond your comfort zone. Engaging with partners who challenge and inspire personal growth can lead to profound fulfillment. Embrace the discomfort that sometimes accompanies growth, for it's often the bedrock of deeper understanding and connection.

As you refine your love strategy, *communication emerges as an essential tool*. The ability to express needs, boundaries, and desires openly ensures that both partners are aligned and moving towards mutual fulfillment. This crucial aspect of a relationship needs constant cultivation. Whether it's through conversations over coffee or exploring new activities together, these shared engagements can fortify the emotional connection and ensure that it remains vibrant.

An often underestimated component of a fulfillment plan is **emotional resilience**. The inevitability of missteps, misunderstandings, and heartbreak in the world of dating can be disheartening. Building a reservoir of emotional strength allows you to navigate these challenges with grace. Rather than retreating into isolation or cynicism, resilience enables you to view setbacks as lessons that enhance, rather than hinder, your journey to fulfillment.

A crucial step in this plan involves regular check-ins with oneself. Much like a business might review its progress towards annual goals, allocate time periodically to evaluate where you stand in relation to your romantic aspirations. Are your relationships aligning with your core values? Are you feeling heard and appreciated? Adjust your strategies as needed, ensuring that your path remains congruent with your deepest intentions and values.

It's also important to consider *the role of technology* in this fulfillment plan. Although technology facilitates connections, it's essential to use it as a tool rather than a replacement for genuine intimacy. Crafting a fulfillment plan means remaining aware of how digital interactions support or detract from your goals. Negotiate a balance where technology enhances communication and connection without overshadowing authentic engagements.

Remember, your fulfillment plan is a living document. As you grow and your expectations shift, allow the plan to evolve. Relationships are not static, and neither should be your approach to finding fulfillment in them. Revisit your aspirations regularly, recalibrating your strategy to accommodate the ever-changing terrain of your heart.

Ultimately, a fulfillment plan isn't about achieving a perfect relationship—one without flaws or challenges. Rather, it's about creating a relationship grounded in reality, rich with emotional texture, and imbued with a sense of purpose that uplifts both individuals. It's about building a shared life that resonates with the kind of love that feels like coming home.

So as you step forward, armed with intentionality and adaptability, remember that the journey of love is as rewarding as its destination. Let your fulfillment plan be not just a guide but a celebration of your commitment to finding and nurturing meaningful connections in this vast, digital world.

Conclusion

As we close this exploration into the landscape of digital dating, we find ourselves at a unique intersection where technology and emotion meet. The chapters we've navigated have brought to light the myriad ways through which modern tools can both complicate and enhance our search for love. It's evident that technology has not only changed how we meet and interact but also shaped our perceptions and expectations of romance. While every swipe, click, and tap offers the possibility of meeting someone special, it also challenges us to stay grounded and self-aware in a fast-paced virtual world.

Throughout this journey, we've encountered the challenges that digital dating can present, from decision fatigue when faced with endless profiles to maintaining authenticity in a space that often celebrates the superficial. Yet, it's precisely this terrain of complications that tests and refines our desire for genuine human connection. This era implores us to reflect on what it means to love genuinely— balancing the convenience of technology with the raw honesty of emotional intimacy. Embracing both, without letting one overshadow the other, becomes our task.

Dating apps and social media platforms may have become integral to our love lives, but they are just tools—a means to enhance, not replace, the organic process of relating to one another. In acknowledging their role, we must also recognize the importance of stepping beyond screens and fostering connections that resonate more deeply. This requires vulnerability, patience, and a willingness to engage with the complex emotions that arise when forging new relationships.

The narratives shared by those who have journeyed through the digital dating sphere and found lasting love remind us of the power of perseverance and adaptability. Each success story offers lessons not only in love but also in the resilience needed to pursue it amid changing times. They illustrate that, while technology can facilitate encounters, the essence of love remains timeless—honesty, respect, and mutual understanding.

Moreover, the themes of diversity and inclusion woven throughout this exploration underscore the importance of broadening our perspectives. In a world where barriers continue to dissolve thanks to technology, there is a compelling call to champion a dating environment that celebrates differences. As more voices are heard and more stories are shared, our understanding of love—including who deserves it and how it's expressed—expands.

In thinking about the future, it's clear that the evolution of digital dating is far from over. Emerging trends and new technologies promise further innovations that will reshape our social landscapes. However, irrespective of what's to come, the human pursuit of connection remains a constant. Our quest for love will always bring us back to the fundamental question: What truly matters in a partner, and how do we cultivate a meaningful bond?

The conversations surrounding therapy and self-reflection in relationships also reinforce the significance of internal work. Whether it's through professional guidance or personal introspection, understanding oneself is paramount when seeking to build a shared future with another. Encouraging a culture that values emotional intelligence and self-awareness can only serve to deepen the connections we form in our personal lives.

As we look ahead, let us carry with us the realizations that, while digital love stories can begin with a swipe or a message, their longevity is rooted in time-honored principles. We are invited to write our own success stories by being intentional, keeping our hearts open, and respecting the journey. By harmonizing technology with authenticity, every interaction becomes an opportunity for learning and growth.

Ultimately, the digital era of romance beckons us to be not just consumers of love, but creators and curators of our own romantic destinies. By crafting a personal love strategy that aligns with our values and desires, we better navigate the complexities of modern dating. This book encourages you to embrace the journey with courage, creativity, and compassion, and to trust that, amid the algorithms and interfaces, a deeply meaningful connection is waiting just for you.

Appendix A:
Appendix

As we've journeyed through the nuanced paths of modern romance in this book, the appendix serves as a treasure trove of additional resources and actionable tools that complement your quest for authentic connections in the digital realm. Here, readers will find curated selections of further reading to deepen their understanding of love in the modern age, complemented by pragmatic tips for honing tech-savvy dating skills. Whether you are a digital native or just dipping your toes into the world of online romance, these resources are designed to inspire confidence and encourage a more mindful approach to building meaningful relationships. We've assembled this collection to not only support your love journey but to empower you to navigate the ever-evolving digital landscape with grace and authenticity.

Resources for Further Reading

Diving deeper into the world of digital dating, you'll find a vast array of literature that can broaden your understanding and sharpen your approach. These resources are invaluable for anyone seeking to explore the subtleties of modern romance further. They span various disciplines, providing insights from psychology, sociology, and even evolutionary biology. This section is designed to guide you to some of the most compelling and thought-provoking readings that complement the themes discussed throughout this book.

For those keen on understanding the psychological underpinnings of digital connections, one might start with books that explore the intersection of technology and human behavior. *The Shallows: What the Internet Is Doing to Our Brains* by Nicholas Carr offers a comprehensive look at how the internet affects our cognitive processes, which can be particularly illuminating when considering how we form connections online. Coupled with Sherry Turkle's *Alone Together: Why We Expect More from Technology and Less from Each Other*, these works explore how digital communication shapes personal relationships and our expectations of intimacy.

Exploring the historical evolution of romance and its adaptation in the digital age can enrich your perspective on current trends. Works like *Romantic Love in Cultural Contexts* edited by Victor Karandashev provide a broader cultural lens on how love and romance have been redefined through varying cultural influences over time. This anthology offers a global perspective, allowing readers to compare and contrast cultural norms, while understanding how globalization impacts romantic practices.

For those interested in the algorithmic side of dating, *Weapons of Math Destruction: How Big Data Increases Inequality and Threatens Democracy* by Cathy O'Neil sheds light on the significant role data plays in shaping our reality, including the online dating landscape. It'll prompt you to think critically about how algorithms influence who you meet and the potential biases embedded within these systems. Further, *Algorithms of Oppression: How Search Engines Reinforce Racism* by Safiya Umoja Noble provides a depth of understanding into how digital platforms can perpetuate discrimination, offering a primer for Chapter 16's discussion on diversity and inclusion.

If your focus leans towards the dynamics of communication and building effective relationships, books such as *Nonviolent Communication: A Language of Life* by Marshall B. Rosenberg offer strategies to foster understanding and empathy in conversations, valuable when translating texting into deeper connections. Additionally, Esther Perel's *The State of Affairs: Rethinking Infidelity* presents a nuanced exploration of commitment and intimacy, both online and offline, addressing complex relational dynamics in the age of digital cross-boundaries.

On the topic of mindful dating, *Emotional Intelligence: Why It Can Matter More Than IQ* by Daniel Goleman provides key insights into how emotional intelligence enhances personal relationships, offering tools to develop mindfulness and presence, crucial in navigating fast-paced digital interactions. For a more practical guide, *Modern Romance* by Aziz Ansari uses humor and research to dissect the intricacies of romance in the age of technology, offering relatable narratives and practical advice.

The societal shifts affecting modern dating are well captured in works examining contemporary cultural changes. *Digital Minimalism: Choosing a Focused Life in a Noisy World* by Cal Newport encourages finding balance and authenticity in a hyper-connected world, resonating with themes from Chapter 13. Likewise, *The End of Love: A Sociology of Negative Relations* by Eva Illouz explores how contemporary cultural and economic transformations impact romantic relationships, providing a critical viewpoint on love's place in an increasingly transactional society.

For women navigating digital dating dynamics, *Lean In: Women, Work, and the Will to Lead* by Sheryl Sandberg can empower and inspire confidence, particularly in settings dominated by underlying gender biases. Complement this with *The Confidence Code: The Science and Art of Self-Assurance—What Women Should Know* by Katty Kay and Claire Shipman to delve into the science behind confidence and its significance in asserting oneself within digital relationships.

Finally, for those curious about the future trajectory of digital dating, *Future Presence: How Virtual Reality Is Changing Human Connection, Intimacy, and the Limits of Ordinary Life* by Peter Rubin offers a fascinating look into how emerging technologies might redefine intimacy and human interaction. This is particularly pertinent as we move into uncharted territories of romance shaped by innovation and technological evolution.

Each of these resources provides a portal into deeper exploration and understanding of the multi-faceted nature of love and relationships in our digital age. Whether you're looking to enhance your empathy, critically engage with the systems in place, or simply become a more informed dater, there's a wealth of knowledge accessible to you. Reflecting upon and integrating these perspectives will undoubtedly enrich your journey in discovering and fostering genuine connections.

Tips and Tools for Tech-Savvy Dating

In today's ever-evolving digital world, finding love is an experience deeply intertwined with technology. With dating apps and social media platforms becoming the go-to methods for meeting potential partners, it's crucial to understand the tools at your disposal to navigate modern dating successfully. From optimizing your online presence to leveraging analytics, these tips and tools can help you create genuine connections.

Let's start with profiles. Profiles are often your first impression, so treat them like your digital calling card. Use clear, recent photos, and craft a bio that's not just about listing facts but sharing stories that reflect your personality. Think humor, sincerity, and brevity. Tools like photo analyzers can rate the effectiveness of your images in making a memorable impact.

Beyond personal photos, consider using virtual tools that enhance your dating profile's visibility. For instance, certain dating apps offer premium services to boost your profile. These features, while not always necessary, can give you a leg-up in crowded markets. Just remember, while technology can enhance opportunities, it's your authenticity that will ultimately win hearts.

Effective communication is the backbone of any successful relationship, and digital dating is no exception. Use messaging tools thoughtfully, aiming for a balance between intrigue and clarity. Utilize features such as voice notes and video calls to add layers to communication that texts can't always achieve. This helps in assessing compatibility more thoroughly before deciding to meet in person.

Moreover, drawing on psychological tools can make your online dating experience more strategic. Understanding behavioral patterns through the lens of psychology can elucidate why certain profiles may appeal more to you than others. Utilize insights about the "Dopamine Effect" to recognize why you might gravitate towards certain dating behaviors, helping you make more intentional choices.

For those looking for deeper insights into compatibility, consider using personality tests or compatibility quizzes available on various platforms. These tools don't just break the ice but can offer meaningful data points about shared values and interests.

Keeping organized amidst the barrage of messages and connections can be challenging. Enter digital organization tools. Apps like note-taking or track-keeping tools help manage interactions and remember details about different people. This ensures that no meaningful conversation gets lost in the shuffle.

Security in digital dating is paramount. Protecting your personal information with savvy tools like VPNs and ensuring your online interactions are secure can provide peace of mind. Familiarize yourself with privacy settings on each platform and regularly update passwords to keep your data safe.

In an era dominated by social media, managing your online image is crucial. Be conscious of how your social media presence might be perceived by potential partners. Tools like audit services help review your profiles across platforms, ensuring you're displayed in the best light, while still being true to yourself.

For tech-savvy daters, utilizing analytics can reveal patterns in your dating experiences. Several apps now provide feedback loops or reports on swiping habits, matches, and interactions. Reflecting on these can offer valuable introspection into your dating preferences and decision-making processes.

Beyond apps, consider the growing impact of virtual reality (VR) in dating. As VR technology becomes more accessible, it offers revolutionary ways to connect. Virtual meetups, dates, or experiences become immersive, breaking geographic barriers and adding novel dimensions to dating.

Finally, lean on communities and support networks. Online forums, webinars, and dating discussion groups can offer communal support and advice. Engaging with diverse perspectives can enhance your understanding of the digital dating scene and introduce new strategies to consider.

The journey of finding love online doesn't have to be daunting. Armed with the right tools and a mindful approach, digital dating can be not just effective but genuinely rewarding. By melding technology with authenticity, you're more inclined to meet someone who resonates with your true self.